Women, Men and Equality

ISSUES

Volume 112

efore

Series Editor

Craig Donnellan

Assistant Editor

Lisa Firth

Independence

Educational Publishers
Cambridge

First published by Independence
PO Box 295
Cambridge CB1 3XP
England

British Library Cataloguing in Publication Data
Women, Men and Equality – (Issues Series)
I. Donnellan, Craig II. Series
305.3

ISBN 1 86168 345 6

Printed in Great Britain
MWL Print Group Ltd

Layout by
Lisa Firth

Cover
The illustration on the front cover is by
Don Hatcher.

CONTENTS

Introduction

Women, Men and Equality is the one hundred and twelfth volume in the **Issues** series. The aim of this series is to offer up-to-date information about important issues in our world.

Women, Men and Equality looks at the topic of gender and education, as well as gender in employment and the issue of gender roles in society.

The information comes from a wide variety of sources and includes:
Government reports and statistics
Newspaper reports and features
Magazine articles and surveys
Website material
Literature from lobby groups
and charitable organisations.

It is hoped that, as you read about the many aspects of the issues explored in this book, you will critically evaluate the information presented. It is important that you decide whether you are being presented with facts or opinions. Does the writer give a biased or an unbiased report? If an opinion is being expressed, do you agree with the writer?

Women, Men and Equality offers a useful starting-point for those who need convenient access to information about the many issues involved. However, it is only a starting-point. At the back of the book is a list of organisations which you may want to contact for further information.

*****

Girls outperform boys at GCSE and A level

Information from the Office for National Statistics

Girls generally perform better than boys at GCSE and at GCE A level (or equivalent) in the UK. In 2001/02, 58 per cent of girls in their last year of compulsory education achieved five or more GCSE grades A*-C, compared with 47 per cent of boys. Forty-three per cent of young women gained two or more A levels or equivalent compared with 34 per cent of young men.

> *Forty-three per cent of young women gained two or more A levels or equivalent compared with 34 per cent of young men*

The difference in achievement between the sexes starts at an early age. In England from key stage 1 (5-7 years old) through to key stage 4 (14-16 years old) girls score consistently higher than boys, though the difference is much less marked in maths and science than in English.

Over recent years there has been an increase in the proportion of both young women and young men in the UK who gain two or more GCE A levels (or equivalent). This increase has been more marked among women. Between 1992/93 and 2001/02 the proportion of women gaining this result more than doubled from 20 per cent to 43 per cent. Over the same period the proportion of men increased from 18 per cent to 34 per cent.

At A level, women outperformed men in virtually all subject groups in 2000/01. With the exception of only General Studies, English Literature and some languages, a greater proportion of women than men achieved grades A-C.

Women also outperform men in vocational qualifications – 29 per cent of young women in schools and colleges gained a distinction for their Advanced General National Vocational Qualification (GNVQ) in 2000/01, compared with 17 per cent of young men.

Although Business was the most popular subject for both men and women taking an Advanced GNVQ, the next most popular subjects differed between the sexes. Twenty-five per cent of women took Health and Social Care compared with 1 per cent of men, whereas 22 per cent of men took Information Technology compared with 4 per cent of women.

Among those who took first degrees in 2002, men and women were almost equally likely to gain a first – 10 per cent of men compared with 9 per cent of women. However, a greater proportion of women achieved an upper second – 49 per cent of women compared with 40 per cent of men.

■ The above information is from the Office for National Statistics. Visit www.statistics.gov.uk for more.
© Crown Copyright

Further education 2003/04:
Learners on LSC-funded FE vision, England

Area of learning	Women %	Men %
Hairdressing and beauty therapy	91	9
Humanities	69	31
Business administration, management and professional	67	33
Arts and media	67	33
Health, social care and public services	66	34
Science and mathematics	62	38
English, languages and communication	62	38
Hospitality, sports, leisure and travel	60	40
ICT	60	40
Foundation programmes	58	42
Construction	6	94
All areas*	**60**	**40**

* including areas not listed above.

Source: Learning and Skills Council (2004) Further Education, work based learning for young people and adult and community learning – learner numbers in England 2003/04, ILR/SFR05.

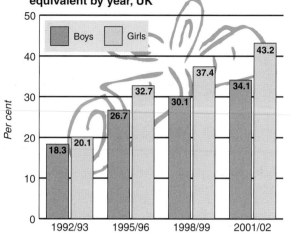

Achievement of two or more[1] GCE A levels[2] or equivalent by year, UK

Boys / Girls

Year	Boys	Girls
1992/93	18.3	20.1
1995/96	26.7	32.7
1998/99	30.1	37.4
2001/02	34.1	43.2

Per cent

1. Equivalent to 3 or more highers.
2. 2 AS levels count as 1 A level pass. Data prior to 1995/9 refer to school pupils only.

Source: Crown copyright

Higher education 2002/03:
First degree undergraduates in HE institutions, Great Britain

Selected subject areas	% Women	% Men
Education	81	19
Subjects allied to medicine	81	19
Languages	72	28
Biological sciences	64	36
Law	62	38
Creative arts and design	61	39
Social studies	58	42
Medicine and dentistry	57	43
Historical and philosophical studies	55	45
Business and administrative studies	51	49
Physical sciences	40	60
Computer science	20	80
Engineering and technology	15	85
All subjects*	**54**	**46**

* including subject areas not listed separately above.

Source: Higher Education Statistics Agency (2004) Students in Higher Education Institutions 2002/03 re-issue.

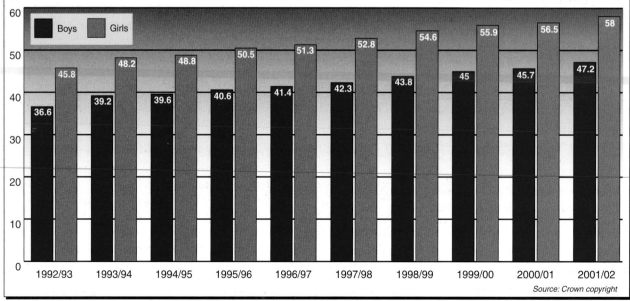

% Pupils achieving five or more GCSE grades A* to C or equivalent, UK, by year

Boys / Girls

Year	Boys	Girls
1992/93	36.6	45.8
1993/94	39.2	48.2
1994/95	39.6	48.8
1995/96	40.6	50.5
1996/97	41.4	51.3
1997/98	42.3	52.8
1998/99	43.8	54.6
1999/00	45	55.9
2000/01	45.7	56.5
2001/02	47.2	58

Source: Crown copyright

What is the cause of boys' underachievement?

Information from the Department for Education and Skills

The gender gap is variously construed as resulting from:

■ girls' greater maturity and more effective learning strategies at all ages, and the apparent success of equal opportunities programmes in schools; the emphasis amongst girls on collaboration, talk and sharing;

■ (some) boys' disregard for authority, academic work and formal achievement, and the identification with concepts of masculinity which are frequently seen to be in direct conflict with the ethos of the school;

■ differences in students' attitudes to work, and their goals and aspirations, linked to the wider social context of changing labour markets, de-industrialisation and male employment;

■ differential gender interactions between pupils and teachers in the classroom, particularly as perceived by (some) boys;

■ the influence of laddish behaviour, the bravado and noise as boys seek to define their masculinity; the inclination of many boys to act in ways in line with peer group norms, in ways which protect their macho image – itself a form of self-defence for many boys; peer group pressure against the academic work ethic, resulting in male behaviour which is less likely to acknowledge and accept boundaries; the influence of personal and social development, including the role of language in boys' achievement. For example, girls have been observed to develop their vocabulary sooner and acquire some language concepts (such as passive voice) earlier than boys;

■ boys' efforts to avoid the culture of failure, to seek explanations – through their off-task behaviour, their lack of effort in terms of class work, homework and course-work, their lack of acceptance of the aims / objectives of the school – for their poor performance in school, to protect themselves against failure and competition; the possibility of failure can lead to anger, hostility and disaffection; a 'can't do/can't win' insecurity leads to a 'won't try/won't play' culture, which leads to a self-sabotaging, anti-learning stance which in turn can be expressed in physical anger, fighting and dominance; such boys are seen to lack self-esteem as learners.

■ The above information is reprinted with kind permission from the Department for Education and Skills. Visit www.dfes.gov.uk for more information.

© Crown copyright

Computers widen gender gap

Computers are widening the gender gap in schools, as boys spend their spare time playing games while girls use them for homework, new government research has found.

The report, carried out for the Department for Education and Skills by academics at Leeds and Sheffield universities, calls on schools to try to 'redirect' boys' use of computers towards school work.

It found that pupils who used computers for their school work scored higher grades in their GCSEs and national tests than those without access to computers at home.

But children – mainly boys – who regularly played computer games achieved significantly lower grades.

The research comes as the latest GCSE figures showed boys are still lagging behind girls in many key subjects.

The academics, working with BMRB market researchers, said their findings reinforced the view that computers are 'boys' toys'.

'Girls were more likely than boys to use home computers for school work, reflecting their more conscientious attitude to study rather than a preference for ICT,' they said.

'This pattern has implications for the gender gap, given that high leisure use was a negative factor for progress.'

Computer games were played every day or at least once a week by 61% of boys compared with 44% of girls. And 70% of boys said they use games consoles every day or at least once a week, compared with just 32% of girls.

The report added: 'Some children pretended they were using the home computer for educational purposes when they were using it for fun.'

Teachers and parents feared pupils would use computers to cheat by cutting and pasting text from the internet.

The academics researched computer use among pupils aged 11, 14 and 16 at 12 English schools, interviewing a sample of 111 children and their parents. They found 89% of pupils had access to computers at home and English was the subject pupils used computers for most often.

29 August 2005

© Guardian Newspapers Ltd 2005

Girls-only education is shaping the future

Information from the Girls' Schools Association

Clarissa Farr, in her article appearing in the Times Educational Supplement, 19 August 2005, discusses the importance of girls' schools in modern society and the role they play in giving young women the chance to learn and excel without pressure or prejudice. She states that in 100 years it will not be possible to look back and say that women played no part in great events thanks to the emergence and growth of girls' schools.

In 1928, writing about the absence of women from recorded history, Virginia Woolf expressed the view that 'by no possible means could women, with nothing but brains and character at their command, take part in any one of the great movements which, brought together, constitute the historian's view of the past'.

Set against this arresting perspective the findings of a survey published recently about the gender gap and a stark contrast presents itself. Of 58 countries, the UK now has the 8th best record in closing the gap between the fortunes of men and women, with particular reference to economic status, political empowerment, health and education. The reason, the study concludes, is the emphasis we place on the education of girls at secondary and higher level.

Less than 200 years ago, few people thought that girls were capable of benefiting from formal education or, if they were, that there was any point in their receiving it. The waste of talent and frustration of instinct that lie behind the silent history of women is captured by Woolf as a powerful image of madness in the same essay: 'any woman born with a great gift (for writing) in the sixteenth century would certainly have gone crazed, shot herself or ended her days in a lonely cottage outside the village, half witch, half wizard, feared and mocked at'.

Nowadays, we hear more and more about the outstanding achievements of girls in all types of school. We have seen The First Women Award which honoured female achievements. And last month, a study revealed that girls outperform boys at A level not only in girls' schools, but in mixed schools as well. The recent Independent Schools' Council census of patterns in independent education, however, confirms that a girl has her best chance of achieving a place at university if she takes A levels in a girls' school. Why is it that girls' schools, the founding institutions, you might say, of all formal education for women, are still so successful in preparing girls academically and socially for a modern, mixed society?

As with many questions about education, the most revealing answers come from the students themselves. In a recent survey of its alumnae, the Girls' Schools Association asked several hundred women, aged from 20 to 90, what they felt they had gained from their schooling. The answers were unequivocal: the opportunity to pursue all areas of the curriculum without pressure or prejudice; the encouragement to develop an inner confidence and self-belief; the certainty that no door need be closed to them; and the enrichment of friendships that have lasted, in many cases, for life. Are these women who have grown up shy or contemptuous of the opposite sex and unable to form healthy adult relationships? Judging from the number of happily married mothers and grandmothers amongst them, not so you'd notice.

Perhaps the most important silent lesson of the girls' schools today, and the one which gives their graduates

...THERE AREN'T MANY WOMEN IN HISTORY...

-HISTORY IS ABOUT TO HAVE ITS EYES OPENED!

the particular confidence to close the gender gap in what is still a male-dominated world, is the acceptance that girls, while properly respectful of the masculine viewpoint, do not need the endorsement of male approval to validate their decisions. In a girls' school, where her classmates are of her own gender and where women hold positions of responsibility as a matter of course, it does not occur to a girl that her views might need to be checked against those of a male authority. A father at my (girls-only) school, himself a vociferous advocate of single-sex education, recently told me with undisguised distaste about the daughter of a friend of his, who had just taken up the violin and whose teenage boyfriend (in the same class) had been 'very supportive'. How had this lovely, independent girl dwindled into a girlfriend, dependent on the approval of Eliot's ' young man carbuncular'?

The growing independence of women, intellectual, social and financial, though approved of in theory, is still regarded with unspoken suspicion. When women organise themselves to make a statement, to assert a view, to be gloriously themselves, it is only a short time before they are labelled 'strident', 'aggressive', 'shrill' or, worst of all, 'unfeminine'. There is, apparently, something repugnant about the woman who says: 'I am confident in myself; I respect you, but I do not need you to agree with me.' Isn't it time we got over this?

Young women growing up in girls' schools today are full of confidence, humour and spirit; they are also as healthily interested in (and interesting to) the opposite sex as young women ever were. Many of them are destined to fall in love, marry and become mothers, as did the generations before them. But the difference

is that steadily and inexorably, they are, in their own way and with their own words, through politics, academia and all walks of public life, writing themselves into the pages of history. In another hundred years, it will not be possible to look back and say that women played no part in shaping great events. And of all the changes in modern society that will have contributed to that enrichment, the emergence, growth and continued health of girls' schools will be among the most celebrated and significant.

Clarissa Farr is the President of the Girls' Schools Association and Principal of Queenswood School, Herfordshire.

■ The above information is reprinted with kind permission from the Girls' Schools Association. Visit www.gsa.uk.com for more information, or see page 41 for address details.
© GSA 2005

Single-sex teaching

Information from the Department for Education and Skills

The DfES has commissioned a team of educational specialists at Homerton College, Cambridge, to pilot a three-year project. Working with schools around the country, it will examine various strategies with a view to recommending models of good practice and guidance for teachers in order to raise boys' achievement. In terms of single-sex teaching in English comprehensive schools their interim findings report that:

There is conflicting evidence over whether examination results are better for pupils taught in single-sex groups

■ Single-sex teaching is used most often in a single subject (most usually English), in year 9 or years 10-11.

■ Its effectiveness can be difficult to evaluate because it is often undertaken on a short-term basis, for just one year or one cohort of students. The initiative for its introduction is usually from the Department concerned, and it is mainly introduced either for pragmatic reasons (gender imbalance in year group or sets) or as a strategy for raising (boys') achievement.

■ In undertaking single-sex teaching, around two-thirds of schools use different teaching strategies, particularly focusing on strategies to motivate boys. There is also some targeting of teachers to groups, and in some cases modifications are made to the curriculum to suit single-sex groups.

■ There is conflicting evidence over whether examination results are better for pupils taught in single-sex groups.

■ Pupils are almost always in favour of single-sex groupings, especially girls.

■ Teacher opinion is often divided, but most acknowledge greater levels of participation in lessons, and increased confidence amongst both sexes.

■ All-boy sets can be difficult to manage, although teachers often feel that behaviour is better in single-sex groups.

■ A lack of staff commitment is the

main reason for discontinuing single-sex teaching.

- Single-sex teaching appears most likely to be successful where staff are fully committed to it, where there is extensive preparation of staff and students before these groupings are put in place, where gender-specific teaching strategies are used and evolve, and where there is an ethos of achievement and discipline within the school.

Pupils are almost always in favour of single-sex groupings, especially girls

OFSTED's last review of research in this area [ISBN 0-11-350102-1] concluded that the apparently superior performance of single-sex (and especially girls-only) institutions in terms of overall measures of examinations results has been largely due to the superior performance of the pupils entering those schools. When the different nature of the intakes to the schools has been taken into account the differences usually disappear.

A small number of studies in other countries seem to suggest that girls-only institutions retain a very modest edge in performance, even when some major differences in the nature of their intakes have been taken into account. It is difficult to tell whether this advantage results from un-measured aspects of their intakes, which researchers have failed to take into account, or from particular ways in which they are organised and teach.

All schools are free to adopt single-sex teaching and those co-educational schools that have been trying it out in certain subject areas have done so in recognition of what they feel are boys' and girls' differing learning styles and their interaction with each other. Opinions vary on its usefulness, some schools are positive that it has helped to improve results for both sexes, others report no noticeable difference.

Research so far suggests that schools succeed where they have taken a holistic approach to tackling gender differences. That could include creating a positive ethos that counters macho anti-school attitudes among boys; literacy strategies targeted at boys' preferred learning styles; performance data analysis and pupil monitoring; the use of mentors and role models and pupil grouping including single-sex teaching for some subjects.

There is little evidence that a one-size-fits-all approach would be effective in all schools and we are, of course, pleased to support schools in whatever system works best for them.

- The above information is re-printed with kind permission from the Department for Education and Skills. Visit www.dfes.gov.uk for more information.

© Crown copyright

Are girls short-changed in the co-ed classroom?

Information from the Girls' Schools Association

Research in both the UK and USA over the last 20 years has indicated that for many girls, a co-ed classroom does not help them to achieve equality, but indeed may depress self-confidence and limit aspirations. Many girls are short-changed by the co-ed classroom.

- **Boys dominate teacher time.** Classroom observations showed that boys answer and ask more questions, hog the teacher's attention and the apparatus, organise themselves more quickly and ruthlessly to their tasks, while girls hang back through shyness or a desire to be helpful and co-operative. Boys are more demanding of teacher's time both behaviourally and academically.
- **Girls are less likely to take intellectual risks and are more passive.** They fear getting it wrong, looking silly, being considered stupid, being judged by their male peers and found wanting. They prefer to solve problems by team working.
- **Subject choices are more likely to be polarised.** In co-ed schools both boys and girls are more likely to choose traditional male and female subjects. This limits choice and aspirations for both boys and girls.
- **Girls tend to lose self-esteem and confidence as they progress through adolescence.** This is made worse if they are constantly being placed under social pressure from boys. A co-ed environment does not always give them the space and security in which to build up their self-esteem and confidence in their own abilities as individuals.
- **Less positive role models for girls.** Co-ed schools do not always provide girls with the necessary positive role models through the teaching staff and the general ethos and philosophy of the school that is so essential for building girls' self-esteem and confidence. This is particularly the case for schools that have gone co-ed but where girls are in a minority. These are essentially still boys' schools with all the male traditions and trappings.
- **Girls mature physically, mentally and emotionally earlier than boys.** Girls and boys mature physically, mentally and emotionally at different ages. In a co-ed environment this is much more difficult to manage. Girls are likely to lose out, as they tend to mature earlier and may well be held back by slower developing boys
- **Girls can have fewer opportunities for leadership roles** in co-ed schools.

- The above information is reprinted with kind permission from the Girls' Schools Association. Visit www.gsa.uk.com for more information or see page 41 for address details.

© GSA 2005

The achievement gap

Girls beating boys in every area before they are five, study shows

By John Clare,
Education Editor

Girls outstrip boys in academic, social, emotional and physical achievement by the age of five, the first national results of the 'foundation stage profile' showed yesterday.

The measures, on a nine-point scale, of how 560,000 children performed against their early learning goals in 13 areas of activity were based on their teachers' observations of them in the classroom and playground between the ages of three and five.

The widest gap between girls and boys – 16 percentage points – was in creative development, a measure of the skills and understanding children need to 'express their ideas, feelings and preferences with all their senses'.

The gap was narrowest – one percentage point – in knowledge and understanding of the world, the goal of which is to be able to 'construct a wide range of objects, selecting appropriate resources, tools and techniques and adapting their work where necessary'.

For example, using scissors, a hole punch and a glue spreader in making a calendar.

On the way to meeting the goal, they had, from the age of three, shown curiosity about living things; recognised themselves in photographs; recorded a favourite song on a cassette; predicted what would happen if ice cream was left in sunshine; designed a party invitation using a computer program and taken a torch apart to find out how it works.

The dominance of girls was most marked in the areas of personal, social and emotional development. They were more likely than boys to be attentive and concentrate well; persevere when trying to solve a problem; understand that they could expect others to treat their needs, views, cultures and beliefs with respect (indicating a 'positive self-image'); take the ideas of others into account; understand what is right, what is wrong, and why, and be able to express a range of emotions fluently and appropriately.

In the area of physical development, girls were also better than boys at recognising the importance of keeping healthy and demonstrating co-ordination and control in large and small movements.

However, the picture was more mixed in the Three Rs.

Girls did better than boys at speaking with confidence and control, showing awareness of the listener; reading complex words using phonic knowledge; and writing simple sentences, sometimes using capital letters and full stops.

Girls outstrip boys in academic, social, emotional and physical achievement by the age of five

The gap narrowed when it came to 'showing an understanding of how information can be found in non-fiction texts to answer questions about where, who, why and how', and was even smaller in the three areas of mathematical development.

These included recognising, counting, ordering, writing and using numbers up to 20; using a range of strategies for addition and subtraction and using mathematical language to describe three-dimensional objects and two-dimensional shapes.

Most striking was how girls establish from the start a dominance that persists throughout school up to A levels, and how early gender stereotypes are formed.

18 March 2005

© *Telegraph Group Limited 2005*

Gender and the early learning goals

Foundation stage profile 2004: percentage meeting or exceeding the early learning goals

	% Girls	% Boys	% Girls advantage
Dispositions and attitudes	69	56	13
Social development	58	47	11
Emotional development	63	50	13
Listening and talking	57	46	11
Linking sounds and letters	41	31	10
Reading	45	37	8
Writing	39	26	13
Counting	59	55	4
Calculating	44	40	4
Shape, space and measures	51	46	5
Knowledge of the world	53	52	1
Physical development	70	58	12
Creative development	59	43	16

Source: Telegraph Group Ltd 2005

Gender and achievement

Analysis by gender

The key trends to emerge in 2004 are:

- Girls progress more than boys on average in English throughout school and across the key stages.
- At Key Stage 1, the difference between boys' and girls' attainment (of the expected level) in English is 8 percentage points. This gap increases over the key stages to 11 percentage points at Key Stage 2, and 13 percentage points at Key Stage 3.
- Girls also progress more than boys in mathematics and science, although the differences are much smaller than those in English.
- At GCSE, girls continue to progress more than boys. The difference between boys' and girls' attainment (5+ A*-C) in GCSE English is as much as 14 percentage points.

Key Stage 1

- Girls outperform boys in English, maths and science at L2 (the expected level) by an average of 5 per cent, although the difference in maths and science is less.
- Boys outperform girls at the higher L3 maths and science by as much as 5 percentage points in maths and just 2 percentage points in science. This continues the trend from 2001.
- There are some signs that the gender gap is narrowing among younger pupils. The gap between boys' and girls' performance in Key Stage 1 reading and writing and in Key Stage 2 writing has narrowed slightly in recent years.

Key Stage 2

- Girls continue to outperform boys in English, with the gap rising to 11 percentage points from Key Stage 1.
- Girls are starting to close the gap on boys at L5+: 4 percentage points gap from boys in L5+

maths; and 1 percentage point gap in science.
- The gender gap has reduced by 2 percentage points in English KS2 writing test from last year.
- The only target area where boys achieved higher in 2004 was at KS2 Maths L5+ by 4 per cent (33 per cent boys, 29 per cent girls) and by 1 per cent in Science L5+ (43 per cent boys, 42 per cent girls). L4 KS2 Maths and Science are the same year.

Key Stage 3

- Gender gap in English rises to 13 percentage points at Key Stage 3. However, the gap has closed by 5 percentage points since 2001 (18 percentage points gap between girls and boys KS3 English attainment).
- Girls now outperform boys in L5+ maths and science and show signs of overtaking in L6+ maths and science.

GCSE

- Girls continue to outperform boys, particularly at the higher grades (A*-C); in 2004 58.5 per cent of girls achieved 5 or more grades A*-C compared to 48.4 per cent of boys.
- The gender gap has reduced slightly by 0.5% since 2001 for those pupils achieving 5 or more GSCE/GNVQ passes at A*-C.

A levels

- While females do better on this measure, the gender gap has narrowed according to provisional statistics for this year. Males have improved slightly more (7.9 average points score) than females (5.7 average points score) between 2003 and 2004.
- For individual GCE A level performance females outperform males (in A-E pass rate) in every subject except Accounting for which the gap is only 0.1 percentage points.

- The overall female pass rate has been higher than the male pass rate since 1992.

Higher Education

- The percentage of HE students who are women has been increasing steadily over recent decades and they now outnumber men: 56 per cent of HE students in 2002 were women, compared to 38 per cent in 1982.
- In terms of participation rates (the numbers entering HE as a percentage of the population) females have higher rates than men: 37 per cent for women, 30 per cent for men.

Women outnumbered men in Higher Education for the first time in 1995, and the proportion has been increasing steadily since then

---

- The latest data on graduates show 56 per cent are women, and that they get better degrees than men – 58 per cent of female graduates get first/upper seconds, compared to 51 per cent of men.
- Women outnumbered men in HE for the first time in 1995, and the proportion has been increasing steadily since then.
- In terms of HE achievement, the gender gap hasn't changed much: in 1995 the proportion of students who got first/upper second class degrees was 51% for women and 44% for men, compared to 58% and 51% respectively in 2003.

- The above information is from the Department for Education and Skills. Visit www.dfes.gov.uk for more information.

Equality issues in education

From 'An Equal Opportunities Guide for Parents' by the Equal Opportunities Commission

As a parent, you will be anxious to ensure that your children are given equal treatment at school. The requirements of the Sex Discrimination Act must be met by schools and local authorities. Here are the key equality issues of interest to parents of school-age children.

Admission

Schools cannot refuse admission to a prospective pupil on the ground of their sex, or to try to maintain a gender balance by admitting one sex but not another when places are limited. In the private sector, if tests are used as part of a screening or selection process, girls and boys must sit identical tests, and the calculation of scores must not be based on the use of different sex norms.

Curriculum

Girls and boys must have precisely the same access to the curriculum. That is, exactly the same amount of subject teaching and the same subject options. Most schools start with this premise, but also aim to ensure a broad and balanced curriculum. A good curriculum is relevant to all pupils; it reflects diversity and cultural heritage; it builds in positive images and positive action to ensure equality of opportunity is met. Timetables can be structured in such a way that real choice exists.

The hidden curriculum

Children learn a great deal at school and not just from formal classroom lessons. What they see around them teaches them as well. Images and pictures in books and on walls; who does what in the school; rules and regulations give clear messages. For example, if all the books are about boys having adventures and girls doing the washing-up this does not provide good role models or a real picture of what life is really like. Thankfully there is a much wider choice of books now available in schools which provide a more stimulating selection to the young reader. There are many ways in which, often unintentionally, differences based on gender can lead to different treatment. This can give the wrong signals about what girls or boys can achieve. Teachers and parents should not expect different behaviour or achievement from girls or boys. Girls should not be expected to be quieter or better behaved than boys. It must not be assumed that boys can make more demands on a teacher's time.

> *Pupils should not be given the impression that there are 'jobs for men and jobs for women'*

Careers guidance

Pupils should have equal access to course option consultation and careers guidance, and the counselling offered must not be discriminatory. Girls and boys should be made aware of the full range of options available and be encouraged to participate in the broad range of work experiences on offer. Furthermore, pupils should be positively encouraged beyond conventional choices. Positive images such as girls in technology should be used to encourage others. Similarly, boys that choose modern languages, home economics or secretarial studies should not be deflected by sexist assumptions. They should also be encouraged without bias. Pupils should not be given the impression that there are 'jobs for men and jobs for women', but should be encouraged to make subject choices and follow career paths which interest them and correspond with their talents. Careers advice and literature must not differentiate between 'male' and 'female' employment. This is important, not only because girls should not be discouraged from many excellent career opportunities in an increasingly technological society, but also because boys will find that many of the jobs traditionally done by men no longer exist, or are few in number. Effective, nonrestrictive course options and careers guidance can expand opportunities, give more young people access to economic ladders and widen opportunities for personal development.

Pastoral care and personal and social development

Pastoral care in schools provides for the emotional, physical and social needs of individual pupils. All adults in a school should work to foster the belief that all people have value in

their own right, and to create a nonthreatening atmosphere that encourages co-operation. Guidance staff offer support to all pupils within their remit, both individually and in groups, and focus particularly on pupils who are socially or emotionally needy or at risk, and those who have encountered discrimination or harassment.

Personal and Social Development (PSD) is a planned programme carried out in secondary schools, aimed at helping pupils to develop positive attitudes and personal and social skills. PSD courses are built on the principles of equality, justice and mutual respect, and focus on issues such as:

- challenging stereotyped assumptions
- raising self-esteem
- fostering positive relationships
- promoting cultural identity
- acting independently and decision making
- taking responsibility for one's actions
- working with others
- leadership.

Discipline

Not only should the disciplinary policy be the same for both sexes, but the same standards should be expected of girls and boys. Responses to disruptive behaviour should be free of bias, and reactions to disruptive behaviour based on stereotypical images should be discouraged. For example, a pupil should not be reprimanded for behaving in what is perceived to be an 'unfeminine' or 'unmasculine' way. If behaviour is praiseworthy or unacceptable, this should be decided regardless of the pupil's sex.

Language

Language, spoken as well as written, is a powerful means of reinforcing or developing attitudes, and consideration should be given to the language used in teaching. The use of gender-dependent words such as headmaster rather than head teacher should be avoided, and attempts should be made to find gender-neutral words, especially when defining occupations, for example, fire-fighter, police officer. The use of sexist terms should

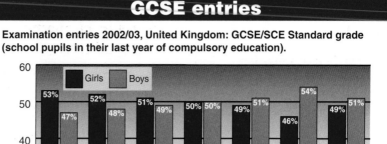

GCSE entries

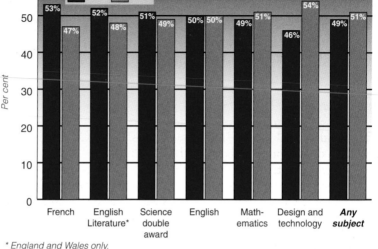

Examination entries 2002/03, United Kingdom: GCSE/SCE Standard grade (school pupils in their last year of compulsory education).

* England and Wales only.

Source: Department for Education and Skills (2004) Education and Training Statistics for the UK 2004 edition.

be discouraged. The school's discipline policy should make it clear that sexist language which uses gender as a form of abuse will not be tolerated.

Requiring girls and boys to wear separate school uniforms may be in breach of the Sex Discrimination Act

---

Teaching materials

All pupils should have unbiased access to school resources and teaching materials. These materials should avoid the depiction of adults in traditional stereotypical roles, and males and females should be equally represented in textbooks, posters and other visual aids. These should represent all sections of society and challenge prejudice, injustice, racist and sexist views. With regard to school equipment, research has suggested that boys dominate the use of equipment in science, technology, design and computer studies. Practices must therefore be in place to ensure that both sexes receive equal hands-on experience.

Accommodation and facilities

Accommodation and facilities provided in school must take account of all pupils. Classrooms should be

safe and stimulating places for everyone. They should also be organised so as to present a welcoming aspect to both sexes. This is particularly important in the areas of science and technology where in the past a 'macho' image or ethos may have been created which was off-putting to many girls. A contrasting environment may have been created in other subject areas such as Home Economics, with similar results for boys. Just as teaching materials should be widely representative of society, the school environment as a whole should portray positive images of all members of society, especially those who are often portrayed negatively, and should challenge stereotypes.

Dress/uniform

Requiring girls and boys to wear separate school uniforms may be in breach of the Sex Discrimination Act. School uniform has tended in the past to be based on male norms, for example the wearing of ties has been expected of both boys and girls. Recent attempts to modernise uniform have favoured a unisex approach with sweatshirts as an alternative. Schools might wish, however, to adopt a less prescriptive approach: if it is simply made clear that pupils are expected to dress in a way that is appropriate, safe and practical, some of the confrontation arising in this sensitive area might be averted.

Extra-curricular activities and sports

Girls and boys must have the same access to all extra-curricular and out-of-school activities, such as chess clubs, hockey clubs or theatre visits. Single-sex competitions in sports are permitted where physical differences between the sexes could disadvantage women or girls. In some schools this has provided legal support for continuing to divide girls and boys into sporting activities traditional to their sex. There is strong evidence, however, that many pupils at both primary and secondary levels are eager and able to participate in a full range of sports, not just in single-sex teams but also in mixed competitive events.

The EOC believes it is wrong that girls who are fit and able to participate in a sport, and capable on their merits to play on teams, should be banned from taking part in the activities they choose. Girls should have the same right as boys to develop their skills. Sport is now the only area of the school curriculum where equality of opportunity is not always provided.

Bullying and harassment

Sexual harassment is not defined in the Sex Discrimination Act, but it can be described as unwanted physical or verbal abuse of a sexual

Only by changing traditional attitudes to 'male' and 'female' areas of the curriculum and making these equally attractive to both sexes will real equality be achieved

nature which adversely affects an individual. The EOC believes that the Sex Discrimination Act extends the unlawful nature of sexual harassment to the field of education. This would mean that an education authority would discriminate against a girl or boy if they did not take steps to prevent the sexual harassment of pupils by teachers.

Bullying and harassment in schools most often occurs when a pupil becomes a victim of other pupils. Bullying of this kind tends to arise from sexual stereotyping of the worst kind, and is based on the popular notions of 'acceptable' male or female behaviour. Boys and girls whose appearance or behaviour does not conform to popular myths are often cruelly victimised by their peers. Schools should ensure that their Equal Opportunities and Bullying Policies make it clear that such behaviour will not be tolerated. Coercion, however, is ineffective if unsupported by good practice. If schools continue to do as much as possible to generate an unbiased culture of mutual respect, it is hoped that incidences of bullying and sexual harassment will decrease, and that, as pupils progress into the adult world, society itself will gradually be influenced in its thinking.

Assessment

Procedures for classroom testing and assessment must not discriminate against pupils on the ground of sex. Girls and boys should be set the same tests, and different sex norms must not be used in the calculation of the test score.

Early intervention

Parents know that children's attitudes are formed at an early age,

and their perceptions about gender are no exception. A recent study of six- and ten-year-olds found that 70 per cent of six-year-old boys wanted to be sportsmen, especially footballers; this rose to 85 per cent by the age of ten. As for girls, 40 per cent of the six-year-olds wanted to be nurses and 30 per cent teachers; at ten years of age roughly one-third wanted to be teachers and the remainder were divided between being flight attendants and hairdressers. Those working with pre-school children should therefore be as vigilant as primary and secondary school staff regarding the provision of a discrimination-free environment in terms of play, books, materials and resources.

Differences between girls and boys in educational outcomes

Sex stereotyping still has a strong influence on course choices made by pupils: greater numbers of boys take technological and scientific subjects, while girls dominate in English and Modern Languages. Given the present skills shortages in the areas of science, technology and information technology, and the growing importance of language skills, it is important that both girls and boys are encouraged into those areas of future employment.

In addition to different academic outcomes, there are disparities in personal development. Some girls leave school with low self-esteem and low expectations. Many boys, on the other hand, leave school inadequately prepared for the expression of their feelings, for the building of personal relationships and for the acceptance and enjoyment of family responsibilities. Once again, these differences can be addressed by tackling inherent attitudes to gender roles. Only by changing traditional attitudes to 'male' and 'female' areas of the curriculum, and by making these equally attractive to both sexes, will real equality be achieved.

■ The above information is reprinted with kind permission from the Equal Opportunities Commission. See www.eoc.org.uk for more or see page 41 for address details.
© EOC

Key facts on women in the labour market

Women's importance in the labour market is growing and the future success of the UK economy depends on women being able to reach their full potential

We want to ensure that women have the opportunity to work when they want and that they can balance work with other family responsibilities.

- There are around 12.2 million women (44%) of working age in employment in the UK, compared to 15.4 million men.
- Women work because they want to – 7 out of 10 mums working full-time say they would work even if they didn't have to.
- Over 50% of mums with children under five work. 44% of lone parents go out to work.
- During March to May 2002, 73% of women aged 16 to 59 were economically active, compared to 84% of working-age men. Women made up 44% of all the economically active. 69% of women of working age were in employment, 159,000 more than a year earlier.*
- 4.5% of economically actively women (575,000) were unemployed during the period, up 36,000 on a year earlier.*
- 5.3 million women (42% of those in employment) worked part-time between March to May 2002. Part-time work is more common for mothers: two-thirds of women with children under 5 who are in employment work part-time.*

(* *Source Labour Force Survey Autumn 2002*)

- Women are less likely than men to be in self-employment: 6.5% of all working-age women in employment are self-employed, compared with 15% of all working age men in employment.

There are around 12.2 million women (44%) of working age in employment in the UK, compared to 15.4 million men

---

- Women comprise around 27% of the 3.5 million self-employed in the UK. It is likely that this figure underestimates women's contribution to enterprise in family businesses and co-ownership.
- Women start up one-third of new businesses and own 13% of all businesses.
- The rate of female self-employment has more than doubled over the last 20 years. (In 1979 only 3.12% of economically active women were self-employed; 6.76% by 1997.)

- Women's participation in self-employment and business ownership is on a par with that of most northern European countries but lower than in the USA (38%).
- The majority of women who set up their own businesses are aged over 35. Many have family commitments; just under half have children aged 16 or under and one-fifth have a child under the age of five.

The UK has the highest female employment rate of the major EU countries and fourth highest of all European Union countries, just behind Denmark, Sweden and Finland. Amongst other European countries, Iceland, Norway and Switzerland all have female employment rates greater than the UK's.

The New Deal for Lone Parents (NDLP) provides support for lone parents who often find it hard to balance work and home life and therefore to return to work. NDLP has supported over 406,480 lone parents and 161,700 jobs have been gained through NDLP (January 2003).

A new mentoring service for lone parents will give lone parents, the majority of whom are women, access to a mentor who will be able to provide confidential support and advice in getting back to work.

- The above information is reprinted with kind permission from the Department for Trade and Industry's Women and Equality Unit. Please visit their website at www.womenandequalityunit.gov.uk for more information or see page 41.

© *Crown copyright*

Sex Discrimination and Equal Pay Acts

The Sex Discrimination Act (SDA) came into force in 1975. The Equal Pay Act (EPA) took effect in 1975. Each act has been amended a number of times since they came into force, the latest amendments to both being in 2003

What do the acts say?

The SDA makes it unlawful to discriminate on the grounds of sex. Specifically, sex discrimination is not allowed in employment, education, advertising or when providing housing, goods, services or facilities. It is unlawful to discriminate because someone is married, in employment or advertisements for jobs. It is also unlawful to discriminate in the employment field on the grounds of gender reassignment. The EPA says women must be paid the same as men when they are doing equal work and vice versa.

What is the EOC?

The Equal Opportunities Commission was created by Parliament in 1976. We have three main tasks:

- working to end sex discrimination
- promoting equal opportunities for women and men
- reviewing and suggesting improvements to the Sex Discrimination Act and the Equal Pay Act. The EOC does not deal with discrimination on the basis of race, age, disability or other grounds.

What does the SDA cover?

The SDA applies to two kinds of discrimination:

- direct discrimination means treating someone unfairly because of their sex
- indirect discrimination means setting conditions that appear to apply to everyone, but in fact discriminate against one sex and are not objectively justifiable.

For example, a rule saying that only people more than 6 feet tall will be hired will exclude far more women than men and will be unlawful sex discrimination unless the employer can show the rule is an appropriate and proportionate way of meeting a genuine business need.

What does the EPA cover?

The EPA applies to pay and other contractual matters where a women and a man are doing:

- like work
- work which has been rated as equivalent
- work which is of equal value.

What are my rights?

Employment
Employers must not discriminate against you because of your sex or because you are married or because you have undergone (or intend to undergo) gender reassignment.

This applies to recruitment, your treatment in your job, chances for promotion and training, dismissal or redundancy. Employers must not label jobs 'for men' or 'for women' except in some very special circumstances: a person's sex can be considered a 'genuine occupational qualification' in jobs such as acting or where the work is mainly or wholly abroad.

Equal pay
Employers must not discriminate against you on the basis of sex, in relation to your pay. For example, if you and another colleague of the opposite sex are doing the same job but you are paid less then you have a right to equal pay – unless the employer can show there is a genuine reason for the pay difference which is not based on sex.

Education
Co-educational schools, colleges and universities must not discriminate in the way they provide facilities or in the way they admit students. For example, all students should have equal access to the National Curriculum. The careers service must not discriminate between boys and girls in the way they provide advice

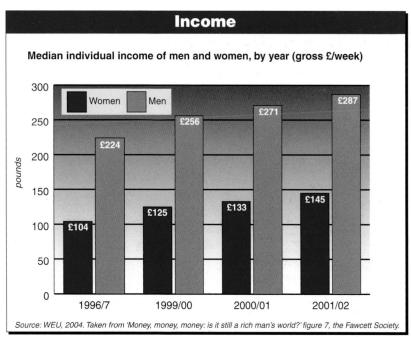

Income

Median individual income of men and women, by year (gross £/week)

- Women
- Men

	1996/7	1999/00	2000/01	2001/02
Women	£104	£125	£133	£145
Men	£224	£256	£271	£287

pounds

Source: WEU, 2004. Taken from 'Money, money, money: is it still a rich man's world?' figure 7, the Fawcett Society.

and assistance. Single-sex schools may restrict admission to boys or girls, but they must not restrict the types of subjects they teach as a result.

Housing, goods, facilities, and services

With a few exceptions, no one providing housing, goods, facilities or services to the public may discriminate against you because of your sex. For example, you must not be discriminated against when:

- applying for a mortgage or loan
- taking part in recreational activities
- buying or renting accommodation.

Advertising

Advertisements must not show that the advertiser intends to discriminate unlawfully. The Equal Opportunities Commission can take legal action against advertisers who discriminate.

Victimisation

You are protected by the law in case you are victimised for trying to exercise your rights under the Sex Discrimination or Equal Pay Acts.

What should I do first?

To help you decide whether to start a case and to gather information on your claim to present your complaint in the best way you may send a Sex Discrimination Act questionnaire to the person you believe has discriminated against you. The questions and answers in this form can be used as evidence in a court or tribunal. The form, SD.74 is available from the EOC or from your trade union, professional association, local employment office, and Jobcentre or unemployment benefit office. There is an equivalent questionnaire for equal pay cases which you can use to find out information from your employer. As well as the EOC or your trade union, you can get a copy of the equal pay questionnaire from the Women and Equality Unit website at the following URL: http://www.womenandequalityunit.gov.uk/pay/update_question.htm.

Where do I take my complaint?

If you feel that you have been treated unfairly because of your sex, marriage or gender reassignment you can take your complaint to a county court, in England or Wales, or to a sheriff court in Scotland. If your complaint is about employment or equal pay you go to an employment tribunal. If your complaint is about education in a state school, college or university you must first give the Secretary of State a chance to exercise the Secretary's powers under the Education Acts.

How soon must I take action?

You must present your complaint of sex, marriage or gender reassignment discrimination to a tribunal not later than three months (minus one day) after the act you are complaining about took place.

You may be able to take a complaint after this time if you can show a good reason that you could not make your complaint earlier.

Complaints about unequal pay can be presented to an employment tribunal at any time while in the job to which your claim relates and up to six months (minus one day) after leaving the job. If you are taking a case to a county or sheriff court you must begin your legal action not later than six months (minus one day) after the act you are complaining about took place.

- The above information is reprinted with kind permission from the Equal Opportunities Commission. Visit www.eoc.org.uk for more information or see page 41 for their address details.

© EOC

Positive discrimination and positive action

Information from the Citizens' Advice Bureau

Positive discrimination

The law against sex discrimination does not allow positive discrimination in favour of one sex. For example, it is unlawful to discriminate in favour of a woman in recruitment or promotion on the grounds that women have previously been adversely affected by discrimination. However, positive action is allowed (see below).

Positive action

The law against sex discrimination does allow positive action in favour of one sex, particularly in training and advertising. Positive action is intended to redress the effects of previous unequal opportunities by providing special encouragement to the minority sex without actively discriminating against the majority sex. Examples of positive action are:

- a training agency may use positive action if it appears that very few or no people of one sex have been engaged in a particular kind of work over the past twelve months
- an employer who has very few, or no employees of one sex engaged in a particular job, or in management positions, may use positive action to provide training for that work to employees of the minority sex only
- a trade union or political party is allowed to use positive action to ensure that members of both sexes are represented at all levels of the organisation. A trade union can, for example, reserve seats on a committee for one sex where it is underrepresented.

- The above information is reprinted with kind permission from the Citizens' Advice Bureau. Visit www.adviceguide.org.uk for more information or see page 41 for address details.

© Citizens' Advice Bureau

Breaking through the Glass Ceiling

Information from the University of Westminster

What is the Glass Ceiling?

This is an imaginary term used to describe the invisible barriers that exist within organisations and which block women from attaining senior executive positions.

How do I break through the Glass Ceiling?

This will be a challenge. The long-term solution is a cultural one both within the workplace and in the wider world outside. Shattering stereotypes of gender roles that perpetuate inequalities between men and women cannot be accomplished by single individuals or in the short term. However, as women continue to slowly break through into senior positions where they can effect organisational change it is more likely that shifts in the perceptions of women at work will occur. So we are back to you, the individual. What strategies can you take to improve your own promotional opportunities?

Understand where the Glass Ceiling starts

The Glass Ceiling is commonly perceived to exist at senior management and executive level. Yet other factors operate to affect career progression at much earlier stages in women's careers. Be aware of the following:

- Women are often channelled into 'people', HR, administrative or research-type functions which are seen in many organisations as secondary or support roles.
- Our own perceptions of what types of work women do, formed by our own local influences, inform our choices.
- Discrimination within organisations limits women's opportunities by 'steering' individuals into the sort of support functions listed above.

UNIVERSITY OF WESTMINSTER

Awareness of these factors will reduce the likelihood of them affecting your career choice.

Women are often seen to lack the leadership skills of a manager

---

Be clear about the areas of work you wish to pursue

Consider the choices you make. Are you doing what you really want to do or just choosing the easy option? Are you being pressured into undertaking a career that maintains the status quo?

Identify opportunities for promotion in the workplace

Do your research. Find out from which department or area managers are traditionally recruited. Allow this

information to inform your choices about which companies to apply to or stay with. Company websites often carry career histories or 'profiles' with staff details.

Develop your skills base

Look out for opportunities, both internally and externally, to broaden your skills base. Identify development opportunities within your field (technical or otherwise) that add extra weight to your portfolio of expertise and which demonstrate to management your commitment to personal improvement.

Develop leadership skills

Women are often seen to lack the leadership skills of a manager. Undertake recognised accredited qualifications in management or leadership so that your skills are formally recognised by an external body. These may be specific qualifications linked to that industry or general qualifications such as the Diploma in Management Studies.

This will help you to address any appropriate criteria when applying for positions at management level.

Find a mentor
Formal mentoring programmes, where staff are paired with more experienced colleagues (often at management level) exist within many organisations. Take advantage of such opportunities. If such schemes don't exist create your own opportunities by contacting members of the management team within your organisation or advising your line manager of your wish for such support.

Build a network
Seek out any internal support or networking initiatives within the organisation that will allow you to build up a network of contacts. Additionally, identify any external organisations that exist to support women within your profession.

Maintain your profile
Regardless of your organisation's promotion policy you need to maintain a profile. How management views you will have an impact on your promotion opportunities. In other words stay visible. Achieving results will not help your career if you stay in the background. Be articulate in meetings; promote the value of your role to decision-makers. Look for opportunities to participate in as many working groups as possible, particularly those with decision-making authority. Identify opportunities to work with other departments to raise your profile with other managers.

Find the right balance
Try not to allow outside commitments to restrict you from taking on extra responsibility. Don't assume that a more senior role will mean you can't maintain a work/life balance.

When applying for promotion identify the time and travel commitments involved and find out whether flexible arrangements, re-prioritising and appropriate delegation would allow you to manage the change.

The Glass Ceiling is commonly perceived to exist at senior management and executive level

---

■ The above information is reprinted with kind permission from the University of Westminster. Visit their website at www.wmin.ac.uk for more information.

© University of Westminster

What is the pay gap and why does it exist?

The gender pay gap refers to the difference in average hourly earnings of men and women

The Government is committed to reducing the gap between men's and women's earnings, and making sure that women's talents are properly used and rewarded.

What is the gender pay gap?
The gender pay gap of 14.4% expresses the difference between men's and women's hourly earnings.

This means that women working full-time are currently paid, on average, 85.6% of men's hourly pay. Since 1975, when the Equal Pay Act came into effect, the full-time pay gap has closed considerably, from 29.5% to 19.8% in 1997 and from 21.2% in 1998 to 18.4% in 2004, using the mean. (There is discontinuity between 1997 and 1998 due to a difference in the methodology of data collection.) Using the

median, the full-time gender pay gap has closed from 17.4% in 1998 to 14.4% in 2004.

There was a decrease in the full-time gender pay gap of 0.2% in 2004 when the median is used and a decrease of 1% when the mean is used. The gender pay gap closed significantly in the South East (by 3.4 percentage points) and by 0.7 percentage points in London. These were the regions where large pay increases amongst highly paid men

last year were behind an increase in the mean measure of the pay gap.

The headline gender pay gap figure is derived from median hourly earnings (excluding overtime) for men and women. Mean figures are often not favoured because they can be affected by changes to the earnings of small numbers of very high-earners.

The part-time gender pay gap is based on the hourly wage of men working full-time and women working part-time, which is defined as being less than 30 hours a week. The part-time gender pay gap for 2004 was 43.2 per cent, as measured by the median – down from 42.5 per cent in 2003. Using the mean, the part-time gender pay gap in 2004 was 40.3 per cent – down from 40.9 per cent in 2003.

The Government is determined to take steps to help, where it can, close the pay gap further.

What are the causes of the pay gap?

Research published by the Government in December 2001 – *The Gender Pay Gap* – authoritatively identifies the key drivers behind the gender pay gap.

It finds that the reasons for the pay gap are complex and interconnected. Key factors include:

- **Human capital differences:** i.e. differences in educational levels and work experience. Historical differences in the levels of qualifications held by men and women have contributed to the pay gap. However, women are still more likely than men to have breaks from paid work to care for children and other dependants. These breaks impact on women's level of work experience, which in turn impacts on their pay rates.
- **Part-time working:** the pay gap between men's and women's part time hourly earnings and men's full-time hourly earnings is particularly large and, because so many women work part-time, this is a major contributor to the gender pay gap. Some of this gap is due to part-time workers having lower levels of qualifications and less work experience. However, it is also due to part-time work being concentrated in less well-paid occupations.
- **Travel patterns:** on average, women spend less time commuting than men. This may be because of time constraints due to balancing work and caring responsibilities. This can impact on women's pay in two ways: smaller pool of jobs to choose from and/or lots of women wanting work in the same location (i.e. near to where they live) which lead to lower wages for those jobs.
- **Occupational segregation:** women's employment is highly concentrated in certain occupations (60 per cent of working women work in just 10 occupations). And those occupations which are female-dominated are often the lowest paid. In addition, women are still under-represented in the higher-paid jobs within occupations – the 'glass ceiling' effect.
- **Workplace segregation:** at the level of individual workplaces, high concentrations of female employees are associated with relatively low rates of pay. And higher levels of part-time working are associated with lower rates of pay, even after other factors have been taken into account.

Other factors which affect the gender pay gap include: job grading practices, appraisal systems, reward

Women working full-time are currently paid, on average, 85.6% of men's hourly pay

systems and retention measures, wage-setting practices and discrimination.

- The above information is reprinted with kind permission from the DTI's Women and Equality Unit. Please visit their website at www.womenandequalityunit.gov.uk for more information or see page 41.

© *Crown copyright*

Gender pay gap wider than previously thought

Information from Incomes Data Services

New earnings figures published by the Office for National Statistics show that the gender pay gap – the gap between average hourly earnings excluding overtime for full-time male and full-time female employees – was 19.5 per cent in 2003 rather than 18 per cent as previously estimated.

In addition, the new statistics show that the gender pay gap has not narrowed as quickly over the six-year period from 1998 to 2003 as earlier figures suggested. According to the new estimates, the gap narrowed over this period by 1.7 percentage points, rather than by two percentage points.

Commenting on these new figures Sally Brett, Assistant Editor of IDS Diversity at Work, said: 'These new estimates, which provide a more accurate picture of the position of men and women in the labour market, show that the gap between men's and women's pay is wider than previously thought. They highlight the persistent inequalities both in pay levels and in access to higher paid managerial and professional jobs. They remind us that much still needs to be done to ensure women are paid fairly and treated equitably in the workplace.'

The latest statistics are derived by applying new methodology to the annual New Earnings Survey, which was the main source of earnings data in the UK, and it is believed they give a better reflection of the actual levels of earnings in the economy.

In particular, the sample used by the NES has now been weighted to make it more representative of the make-up of the actual workforce. This has an impact on the gender pay gap because survey returns from high earners in managerial and professional jobs, who are more likely to be male, are given larger weights because they tend to have lower response rates, and were therefore previously under-represented in the sample compared to people in other occupations.

20 July 2005

- The above information is reprinted with kind permission from Incomes Data Services. Visit www.incomesdata.co.uk for more information.

© *Incomes Data Services*

Women at the top

Women in management [1]

- Women comprise 30% of managers in England, 29% in Scotland and 33% in Wales.
- Managerial occupations remain strongly gender-segregated. While women make up 73% of managers in health and social services, they only make up 6% in production.
- Women's representation also varies by sector. While 40% of managers in the public sector are female, in the private sector it is just 28%.
- Data from the National Management Salary Survey in 2001 revealed that the average female manager earned £34,789, while the average male manager earned £40,289. Women managers therefore earned around 86% of the average annual managerial salary of men.

Women in the boardroom [2+3]

In all UK listed companies:

- Less than 1% of chairs are women.
- 4% of executive director posts (including Chief Executive Officer) are held by women.
- 6% of non-executive director posts (employed largely to offer strategic, specific and objective advice at board meetings) are held by women.
- Overall, 4% of directorships are held by women.

In FTSE 100 companies:

- Just over one in ten non-executive posts and one in 40 executive posts are held by women.
- Only one company had a female Chief Executive Officer, in 2002.
- Only 7.2% of directorships are held by women and 39 firms have no female directors.
- 16 of the top 20 FTSE companies had women directors, but only eight of the bottom 20 firms.

Women in politics [4+5]

Parliament

- The 2001 General Election returned 118 women MPs to the House of Commons, a decrease of two from the previous election.

Women represent 17% of all MPs.
- There are 12 minority ethnic MPs, two of whom are women.
- 24% of British members of the European Parliament are female.
- 33% of Cabinet Ministers are women.
- In April 2002 32% of Ministers in the Scottish Parliament, 63% of Ministers in the National Assembly for Wales and 37% of Ministers in the Northern Ireland Assembly were women.

Local government

- In 2001, there were 36 women chief executives in England and Wales out of a total of 351 local authorities.
- In May 2001 29% of local councillors were women and 2.5% of councillors were of ethnic minority origin.

Women in the Senior Civil Service [4]

- Women comprise 24% of civil servants at the Senior Civil Service level.

Women in the police force [1]

- 7% of Chief Constables and 9% of Assistant Chief Constables are women.

Women in judiciary [6]

- 6% of High Court Judges are women – six out of a total of 107. There are no High Court Judges from a minority ethnic background.

- 21% of District Judges (Magistrates' Courts) are women – 22 out of a total of 105. Of these women, 5% are from a minority ethnic background.

Women in public appointments [7+8]

- 34% of all the boards of non-departmental public bodies, nationalised industries, public corporations and health bodies are held by women.
- 2.3% of all national and regional public appointments are held by minority ethnic women.

NHS trust chairs

- Almost 40% of NHS trust chairs are women.
- Just under 7% of chairs are from an ethnic minority.

Sources

1 *Women and Men in Britain: Management*, EOC, 2002
2 *Review of the role and effectiveness of non-executive directors*, Derek Higgs, January 2003
3 *The 2002 Female FTSE report: Women Directors Moving For-ward*, Dr Val Singh and Professor Susan Vinnicombe, Cranfield School of Management, November 2002
4 *Key indicators of women's position in Britain*, Dench et al, WEU, November 2002
5 *Room at the Top? A Study of Women Chief Executives in Local Government in England and Wales*, Pam Fox and Mike Broussin, Bristol Business School, undated
6 The Lord Chancellor's Department, January 2003
7 Public Bodies 2002
8 Department of Health, February 2002

- The above information is reprinted with kind permission from the Department for Trade and Industry's Women and Equality Unit. For more see page 41 or visit www.womenandequalityunit.gov.uk
© Crown copyright

Women to hold 60% of UK wealth by 2025

Research carried out for Liverpool Victoria

Women will become the UK's financial powerhouses, owning 60% of the nation's personal wealth by 2025, due to the rise of a cohort of financially sophisticated younger women adding to the traditional sources of female wealth such as marriage and inheritance. The research, carried out by the Centre for Economics and Research for the Liverpool Victoria Friendly Society, found that women currently own 48% of the nation's personal wealth.

UK millionaires aged under 45 and over 65 are more likely to be women than men

The predicted change is due to women performing better in secondary, further and higher education than men, higher levels of home ownership among single women than single men, and longer life expectancy for women. These factors combined will see the growth of an influential cohort of financially powerful women in the coming years.

The research also finds that UK millionaires aged under 45 and over 65 are more likely to be women than men. There are 25% more women millionaires aged between 18 and 44 (47,355 women compared with 37,935 men), while women millionaires over 65 years old outnumber their male counterparts by 71,369 to 67,865.

Women's better performance in education and their higher life expectancy are key factors that will drive their rise to the top of the financial tree over the coming years: 58% of girls achieved five or more GCSEs compared with 47% of boys; 43% of girls left school with at least two A levels, compared with 34% of boys; and 1.3 million girls entered higher education and 3.1 million entered further education, compared with 1.0 million and 2.2 million boys respectively.

Women currently have life expectancy of 81 years, compared with men at 76.6 years – this means that wives are more likely to inherit from their husbands than vice versa and that single women have to be more aware of the need to save.

One effect of women's greater success in education is their improved position in the workplace, where more women are assuming higher skilled roles. According to the research, there are higher percentages of women employed in managerial and professional roles compared with previously. Although men still earn more on average than women, the pattern is changing and women's ratio of gross hourly earnings for full-time employees is now 82% of men's – a rise from 63% in 1970.

The research has also revealed that young and elderly women are more likely than men to live on their own and are also more likely to own property than their male peers. This will be another key driver of women's future financial success, and these two age groups are well placed to benefit from any increasing equity value in property in the coming years. The research shows that 63% of 20- to 24-year-old women live away from their parents, compared with just 44% of men. Between the ages of 65 and 75, 34% of women live alone compared with only 19% of men. The percentages rise when these groups reach 75 years of age due to women's higher life expectancy, with 60% of women over 75 living alone compared with just 29% of men.

■ Research published by Liverpool Victoria, carried out by the Centre for Economics and Business Research. For more information visit www.liverpoolvictoria.co.uk and www.cebr.com

© CEBR Ltd 2005

Do our daughters really have the world at their feet?

Information from the Work Foundation

Take Your Daughters to Work Week is a good opportunity to expand the career horizons of young women, but the reality they may face in the workplace could be less attractive. Despite legislation and a greater number of females in the working population, the Work Foundation believes women still face wage inequality; stunted opportunities and career slow tracking.

The Work Foundation welcomes the opportunity the Guide Association is offering young women to meet potential future employers and explore their career options. However, should we really be telling them that they have the world at their feet?

From the age of 20 women can expect to earn 19% less than men

---

7 March 2005 sees the start of Take Your Daughters to Work Week. This scheme, run by Girlguiding UK for the last ten years, is designed to break down barriers to male-dominated careers such as engineering, mechanics and ICT and to challenge organisations in the UK to re-read their female friendly policies and see how they work in the real world.

The current state of work in the real world is not one that we would want our daughters to have to face:

Pay gap
From the age of 20 women can expect to earn 19% less than men, this hasn't changed for the last 10 years. It is exacerbated once you have a family. Even in senior positions women get paid less than men. Women do the majority of low-paid jobs.

Glass ceiling
Working women report being excluded from social networks, having

limited role models and fewer opportunities for management positions.

Glass cliff
Women are more likely to be offered senior roles in failing companies, setting them up for criticism.

Family penalty
Women still bear the brunt of caring and housework, spending double the amount of time as men on household chores and losing out on pay. When our daughters are in work, will they still find it difficult to manage long hours and be mobile?

Old age poverty
Taking time out to care for a family, reduced earning power and jobs in sectors with poor pension provision will lead to reduced economic independence for women. Women are more likely to be poor in old age than men; for every £1 a man receives from a pension a woman receives 32p.

Even though organisations are starting to respond to the needs of a diverse workforce, much more needs to be done. Alexandra Jones, Senior Researcher at the Work Foundation, suggests organisations can help in the following ways:

Encouraging girls at an early age
Choices at GCSE and A level can affect young women's future career choices and pay. By hosting events such as 'Take Your Daughter to Work Day' traditionally male-dominated organisations such as engineering and ICT can encourage more women to apply.

Equal pay audit
Organisations can ensure they are paying their staff fairly by conducting an audit and having an open pay and reward system.

Flexible working
Organisations should ensure this is a genuine option and not a way of separating 'the men from the boys'. Performance management should focus on an individual's outputs and not how often they are in the office.

Don't rely on networks
When considering promotions and recruitment, organisations should not rely on who candidates know. It is difficult for women with family commitments to participate in after-work socialising and be part of 'old boys' or 'golf club' networks. Recruitment and promotion policies need to be transparent and consistent.

Pension provision
Both employers and government should work toward flexible and affordable pension provision that doesn't penalise those who have to take time out to perform other roles.

Alexandra Jones of the Work Foundation concludes: 'Take Your Daughter to Work Week is a wonderful opportunity to show young women how work works. But the problems of the pay gap, the pension gap and the flexible working stigma will not just disappear. The workplace needs to change or our daughters will face similar barriers to their mothers and the workforce will still be failing to maximise the productivity of a large part of the workforce.'
3 March 2005

■ Information from the Work Foundation. See page 41 for address details or for more information visit www.theworkfoundation.com

Free to choose?

Vocational education and training system failing girls

Britain is failing to provide real opportunity and choice for young people entering training and work, according to a report published today (18 July 2005) by the Equal Opportunities Commission (EOC). And girls from lower socio-economic groups are losing out the most.

The *Free to Choose* report reveals that young people – particularly girls from lower socio-economic groups – are not being given the access to careers advice, work-experience placements and training opportunities that would give them true freedom to fulfil their ambitions and potential and gain higher pay. Instead, too many are being channelled into jobs traditional to their sex. By contrast, girls who have entered work through higher education have broken into new, higher-paid jobs in areas like medicine and law and now form more than half of entrants.

80% of girls and 55% of boys said that they would or might be interested in learning to do a non-traditional job

---

Free to Choose is the final report from the EOC's groundbreaking investigation into sex segregation in training and work.

The EOC has found real evidence of support for change among young people:

- 80% of girls and 55% of boys said that they would or might be interested in learning to do a non-traditional job;
- When exploring what would tempt them to try non-traditional work, three-quarters (76%) of girls and 6 in 10 boys (59%) said that they would like to try work normally done by the opposite sex before making a final job choice;

- 25% of boys said caring work sounded interesting or very interesting and 12% of girls were interested in construction; however, less than 3% of childcare apprenticeships are male and less than 2% of construction apprenticeships are female
- 92% of women and men said that they would want children who are about to enter the workforce to be able to make job choices without worrying about traditional stereotypes of women's and men's working roles. 100% in Wales.

Despite this, the EOC found that:

- Only a sixth (15%) of young people received any advice or information on work experience in a sector with a workforce currently dominated by the opposite sex;
- In one survey, of the 45 childcare work-experience placements undertaken, only 2 were filled by boys, whereas only 29 of the girls had listed it as their future choice;
- Some young people reported being actively discouraged to pursue a career outside the norm for their sex. One female trainee plumber said: 'schools careers – it would have been good if they had just not discouraged us';

- 67% of women didn't know when they chose their career about the often lower pay for work mostly done by women and of these two thirds of young women said they would have considered a wider range of career options had they known;
- Apprenticeships are perpetuating gender segregation or even making it worse.

Although boys are affected by restricted choices, the situation has a particularly damaging effect on girls because jobs with a mostly female workforce offer much lower rates of pay than those where the workforce is mostly male: salaries for those employed in childcare are half or less than in areas such as engineering and plumbing.

The EOC is today launching a new interactive website – www.works4me.org.uk – to help young people find out more about the full range of career options.

The investigation also found a clear correlation between skills shortages and those sectors with few women. The *Free to Choose* report also shows that many employers want to take on a more diverse range of recruits:

- 7 in 10 (70%) employers surveyed by the EOC thought atypical recruits could bring positive benefits to their business;
- 8 in 10 said a better gender mix would create a better range of skills and talents.

Julie Mellor, Chair of the EOC, said: 'Girls from lower socio-economic groups are often ending up in lower-paid work than boys, despite doing well at school. Opportunities for some boys to take up the work that suits them are also being blocked. Britain can't go on letting young people down – the choices they make at an early age affect their whole lives and the economy suffers if employers can't get the right mix of skills and talents.

'Our findings demonstrate how important it is for Government to

remove the barriers facing young people and the employers who want to take them on – with careers advice available to every child, including information on non-traditional work and its pay, the chance of two work-experience placements, one non-traditional; and apprenticeships which open doors to more non-traditional trainees. Tackling occupational segregation needs to be put at the heart of Government's strategy to raise skills and productivity.'

Ruth Kelly, Secretary of State for Education and Skills, who is speaking at the EOC's launch event, said:

'I welcome the publication of this report. The links between occupational segregation, national and employer productivity, skills shortages and the gender pay gap are particularly striking. It is clear that these issues need to be addressed, both for the benefit of our economy and on social justice grounds.

'Occupations with high levels of skill shortage vacancies very often have gender imbalances. For example, 6% of all skill shortage vacancies are in skilled construction occupations – where 99% of the workforce is male. Conversely 7% of skill shortage vacancies are in personal service occupations within Health and Social Work – where 90% of the workforce is female.

25% of boys said caring work sounded interesting or very interesting and 12% of girls were interested in construction

---

'Our recent 14-19 and Skills White Papers contain many proposals which should help address the EOC's concerns. These include improving the quality and range of information, advice and guidance available to teenagers and adults, and the aim of creating a truly comprehensive education system.'

Patricia Hewitt, Secretary of State for Trade and Industry, said:

'The Government is committed to ensuring that young people from all backgrounds get to achieve their full potential and get the job they want. The recently published Skills White Paper will ensure that young women and men get the skills needed to join the workforce and contribute to the UK's competitiveness in business.'

More information can be found at www.eoc.org.uk/segregation
18 July 2005

■ The above information is reprinted with kind permission from the Equal Opportunities Commission. Visit www.eoc.org.uk for more information or see page 41.

© 2005 Equal Opportunities Commission

Women's job satisfaction

Women are no longer happy in their work, says study

Women's job satisfaction is in decline for the first time, even though the opportunities open to them are unparalleled, Government-funded research showed yesterday.

Having historically enjoyed work more than men, women are now just as disillusioned, says a report by Prof Michael Rose of Bath University.

Those who work part-time, many of whom combine motherhood with a career, are particularly dissatisfied. Their job satisfaction has 'collapsed', he said.

Part-time women workers were once thought of as 'grateful slaves' in a pin-money underclass, happy to take low-grade jobs for poor pay and conditions, Prof Rose said.

'If women ever had such attitudes they certainly don't have them now. And you can forget the "pin-money" tag. OK, these women are not career builders like many of the full-timers. But more and more see themselves as sharing the role of breadwinner.

By Sarah Womack, Social Affairs Correspondent

'They are more critical of their jobs because they share the provider role.'

Prof Rose's research is based on the British Household Panel Survey, regarded as one of the most authoritative studies in the world.

The level of job satisfaction among all females has been falling for 15 years. For men it has stayed the same

---

It traces the attitudes and behaviour of a representative sample of 5,000 households, involving 10,000 individuals.

Prof Rose says the study shows the level of job satisfaction among all

females has been falling for 15 years. For men it has stayed the same.

Historically, women have been happier at work, a finding thought to have reflected their lower expectations.

The women surveyed for Prof Rose's study covered 371 occupations, ranging from secretaries to chief executives of multi-national organisations.

They were asked about pay, job security, training, hours of work and fringe benefits. The women were asked to score the issues from one to seven.

'The average score for overall job satisfaction among part-time women in the UK has fallen by eight per cent since the early Nineties and among full-time women by three per cent,' said Prof Rose, who specialises in economic and social research. 'The fall among men is zero.

'These figures may not seem huge but it's like politics. A lead of four per cent is enough to get you elected.

The figures have to be read in that sort of way.'

Some commentators argued that women felt increasingly stressed at work, suffering a serious drop in their general sense of well-being.

But Prof Rose, who carried out the research for the Economic and Social Research Council, rejected this.

'There's no sign of a general fall in psychological well-being among women,' he said.

'Our measures of general happiness – general well-being outside the workplace – show a slight upward trend.

'It is possible to be happy with your life and totally cheesed off with your job.'

He said that one explanation of why women had become so disillusioned was that they were being driven out to work for economic survival rather than personal satisfaction.

'They work because they are helping to pay mortgages and are involved more closely with providing money to the household. Men are no longer looked on uniquely as the "providers".

'Women are taking a tougher look at what they are doing and asking "Am I getting a good deal from my employer? Could I do better somewhere else?"'

His findings, presented at the Social Policy Association Annual Conference in Bath, come as the Government spends millions of pounds encouraging women back to work after having families.

However, many also do the majority of the child care and housework and say they find it hard to juggle domestic commitments with employment.

28 June 2005

Jobs for the boys?

Equal Opportunities Commission research reveals untapped resource of men to fill childcare skills shortage

Nearly three in ten men (27%) would consider working in the childcare sector, and one in four boys expresses an interest in entering the 'caring' professions – yet only one in fifty childcare workers are men, a new report released today (12 September 2005) by the Equal Opportunities Commission (EOC) shows.

Men's interest in childcare may be linked to the increasingly active role of men as fathers. Previous research released last month by the EOC shows that 4 out of 5 new fathers said they would be happy to stay at home and look after their child, and 9 out of 10 were as confident as their partner at looking after their baby.

The EOC's report, *Men Into Childcare*, which includes a review of evidence and current activity to recruit men to the sector, is released at a time when the Government needs to attract more men into childcare to deliver on its promise to further expand childcare. The Department for Education and Skills estimates it will need a further 163,000 workers over the next few years – increasing the size of the current childcare workforce by more than fifty per cent. Furthermore, though there is now one place for every four children under eight – a significant improvement from one for every nine children in 1997 — parents still often report difficulties in finding suitable local childcare.

Children also stand to benefit. The EOC's research shows that a more diverse workforce significantly improves the quality of childcare by exposing children to a wider range of positive role models. The majority of parents support bringing more male childcare workers into the profession – over three-quarters (77%) of respondents to a MORI survey were in favour of more male carers.

The EOC has identified the following key barriers to recruiting men into childcare:
- Low pay, poor terms and conditions
- The perception of childcare as being 'women's work' and a belief that men are unwelcome
- Insufficient information for boys at schools on caring careers and apprenticeships, despite high levels of interest.

The EOC is calling for the Government to act to:
- Raise the status of the caring profession through qualifications and an emphasis on training,

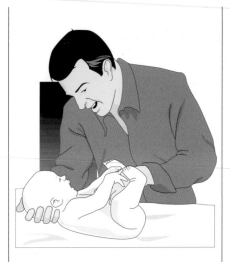

which, in turn, should result in better pay for both men and women in the profession

■ Provide better information for young people about non-traditional career options

■ Make non-traditional work experience placements for boys and girls more widely available.

Jenny Watson, Acting Chair of the EOC, said:

'Childcare services, particularly the new plans for extended schools, will not meet parents' needs if they can't recruit enough staff – and they can't do so unless they recruit men. We know that men are interested in working with children, with nearly a third of men saying they'd think about the childcare sector as a career. We know that children benefit when more men are involved. And we know that more than three-quarters of parents would like to see more men working in their children's nurseries, play centres and after-school clubs. So it's time to start dismantling the barriers that stand in men's way.

'We're pleased that the Government's recently published Youth Green Paper has heeded our call to improve careers advice, but more is needed. Boys need to be given careers advice and support to attract them into childcare, and allowed to make their choice of career without the bias and prejudice of others shaping their decision. But in the longer term, the status of the profession needs to be raised through better pay and conditions. Working with children is a rewarding and important job. It needs to be given the status and financial benefit it deserves.'

Thom Crabbe from Daycare Trust said:

'We welcome the authoritative voice of the EOC in reviewing and bringing renewed attention to the important issues around men in childcare. The issue needs to be firmly located in discussions about gender roles, equality and careers in caring. We need to build on the best examples and successes around the country and to tackle the tough issues firmly and clearly. Men in childcare matter for children, good for services and beneficial for society.'

Notes

Key facts from the EOC's report *Men Into Childcare*:

■ Men are only 2-3% of the childcare workforce at a time when more workers are needed to support the Government's 10-year plan to expand childcare, including the creation of 'extended schools' to provide childcare before and after the school day and during holidays.

■ There are untapped levels of interest in caring work from young men and adults: 25% of young men say they are interested or very interested in caring work (survey of 1,300 girls and boys in year 10), and men are turning to childcare as a second-chance career.

■ Men comprise 10% of after-school care workers, signalling potential positive returns from focusing on recruiting men to support extended schools initiatives.

■ We are losing out on the recognised benefits of more men in childcare.

■ Employers say that recruiting more men would improve the image of the childcare sector, be good for business and help address the skills shortages.

■ Practitioners believe more men enhance the quality of childcare.

■ The majority of parents are in favour of men working in childcare. Barriers to recruiting more men include:

■ Boys at school are not being given information on caring careers or apprenticeships, despite high levels of interest.

■ The undervaluing of childcare – low pay, poor terms and conditions, few opportunities for progression, the low status of childcare and its perception as 'women's work' that is linked to mothering.

■ The predominance of part-time work.

■ Reliance on marketing and advertising childcare work to men is proving insufficient on its own: a range of measures is needed.

In Denmark men are 8% of the workforce; recruitment campaigns attract men and childcare workers are trained 'pedagogues' able to work with a range of children. Norway has a target of 20% male childcare workers by 2010.

12 September 2005

■ The above information is reprinted with kind permission from the Equal Opportunities Commission. Visit www.eoc.org.uk for more information or see page 41.

© 2005 Equal Opportunities Commission

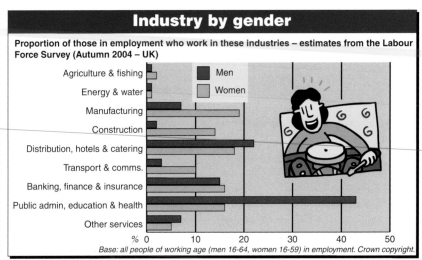

Industry by gender

Proportion of those in employment who work in these industries – estimates from the Labour Force Survey (Autumn 2004 – UK)

- Agriculture & fishing
- Energy & water
- Manufacturing
- Construction
- Distribution, hotels & catering
- Transport & comms.
- Banking, finance & insurance
- Public admin, education & health
- Other services

Men / Women

% 0 10 20 30 40 50

Base: all people of working age (men 16-64, women 16-59) in employment. Crown copyright.

Sisters are 'building it for themselves'

Construction industry launches £1 million campaign to attract graduate and female recruits

The construction industry today (18 April 2005) launches a £1 million campaign to attract women and those from black and minority ethnic groups into the industry. The twelve-month Positive Image campaign is fronted by T4 presenter June Sarpong.

It aims to communicate the benefits of a construction career to those most discouraged by its image of 'blokes, bums and bricks'. The campaign will have an emphasis on bringing graduate-level recruits into the industry.

Recent research by the Equal Opportunities Commission shows that while one in eight girls are keen to work in the industry, just 1% of construction workers is female.*

> *The campaign aims to communicate the benefits of a construction career to those most discouraged by its image of 'blokes, bums and bricks'*

'The construction industry is missing out on much-needed talent due to an outdated image that's a real "turn-off" for women and those from ethnic minorities,' says Nicola Thompson, Director of Communications at CITB-ConstructionSkills. 'Like other industries, construction is moving with the times, and this campaign is an investment in its life-blood.

'The industry has openings for professional and graduate-level entrants: from civil engineers to landscape architects. It has developed a need for more technically qualified employees as changing building techniques demand greater science-based skills of its work-force.

'All of this means the brightest and best recruits will find fantastic career opportunities in construction, with upcoming building projects such as the £63 million Thames Gateway development, the £400 million Olympic bid, as well as new schools, hospitals and roads. Construction is growing rapidly and needs 86,000 new people, in craft, technical and management roles this year.'

The 'Positive Image' campaign highlights the best of new British construction design. It features projects from Birmingham's Selfridges building to the Millennium Stadium and the Gateshead Bridge. It showcases the diverse roles that young women and those from black and ethnic groups could be playing in such iconic projects.

The construction industry has a particular need for recruits with engineering, surveying, project management and computer science-related skills. It is also looking for management talent: for those with skills from HR and communications to finance and training.

Aspects of the Positive Image campaign 2005 include:
- The launch of a £1 million grant scheme for undergraduates, Inspire Scholarships, which offers 60 students a year up to £9,000 to help fund their studies, as well as providing scholars with on-site experience.
- National Construction Week (6-13 October 2005), a nationwide campaign in which construction industry employers offer compelling opportunities for local young people and school children to experience construction, for example visiting live building sites to get a first-hand view of the many processes involved in construction.

Nicola Thompson concludes: 'Although latest figures from UCAS show that the number of places accepted on construction degree courses has seen a huge increase on last year, we need to see more new recruits at all levels.

'The Positive Image campaign will showcase the diverse roles that young women and those from black and ethnic minorities could be playing in the next generation of new projects: from rebuilding the nation's school buildings to helping restore heritage buildings.

'A career in the modern construction industry really can take young people to places they never imagined.'

Notes
* March 2005 research from the Equal Opportunities Commission found that:
- Girls from lower social groups are denied access to careers advice, work experience and training.
- Last year just 22 young women in England took up plumbing apprenticeships compared with more than 3,000 young men.
- One in eight girls were keen to work in the construction industry, while one in four boys expressed an interest in care work.
- Only a sixth of young people received advice on work experience in areas dominated by the other sex.

18 April 2005

- The above information is reprinted with kind permission from CITB-ConstructionSkills. Visit www.citb-constructionskills.co.uk for more information or see page 41.

© CITB-ConstructionSkills

Jobs for the girls

Don't get pigeon-holed into careers that are supposedly gender-specific – break the barriers and turn your talents to these traditionally male-dominated roles. By Jane Smith, Careers Expert

Plumber

If you are a practical person and don't mind getting your hands dirty, maybe you should tap into the growing demand for female plumbers. In the past, women faced many barriers when trying to enter this trade: we're not strong enough, the work is sometimes messy, there are no women's loos on a building site. But the huge skills crisis in manual trades has changed all that – so it's definitely a career with a future. There will always be a demand for women in this career because many female householders appreciate having a woman plumber. If you're good, people will use you – it doesn't matter what gender you are.

You can get into this line via a full-time plumbing course or an employed-status Modern Apprenticeship. Your apprenticeship would entail working with an employer and attending a training centre on a part-time basis. The first step would be to identify a plumbing business within your area that can provide the necessary work-based training and experience. Look at the Sum-

handbag ⌽

mitSkills website to find your local Approved Plumbing Centres.

The Institute of Plumbing has a Women in Plumbing group, which aims to raise awareness of career opportunities open to women in the industry and to encourage more women to train as plumbers.

Hospital consultant

Despite the recent upsurge in the numbers of women entering medical schools, it seems that females are still heavily outnumbered in hospital surgical and medical roles. Why is it that women are far more likely to become GPs than to gain positions as consultants? One answer is that because women think of themselves as less technically skilled than men, they tend to specialise in areas with relatively poor prestige and low financial rewards. The 'macho' culture is another reason why women are underrepresented in leading positions in medicine. The men who

make decisions about hiring tend to select candidates whom they see as being tough and decisive – just like themselves. If things go on as they are, hospital consultants will be recruited from a decreasing number of male medical-school graduates.

The times they are a-changing, however, and there has never been a better moment for women to aspire to become hospital consultants. There is a realisation that it is vital to attract the graduates with the highest talent for medicine or surgery, regardless of gender.

If you're good, people will use you – it doesn't matter what gender you are

---

If you are a medical student interested in a career in surgery, you will find it useful to join WIST (Women in Surgical Training). WIST works to enable women who have chosen a career in surgery to realise their professional goals.

Stockbroker

When a woman asked to become a member of the Stock Exchange in the 1970s, she was told it was impossible because there were no ladies' lavatories. Although it's 30 years since the first woman joined the Stock Exchange, attitudes have not changed much, judging from the number of discrimination cases!

The life of a female stockbroker is tough: you need lots of stamina, nerves of steel and bucketloads of confidence. On the plus side, the pay is excellent, you work with a close-knit team and there's a tremendous buzz from dealing with billions of pounds, euros and dollars every day.

A stockbroker's job is to invest money on behalf of clients, so you'll need to be constantly aware of the fluctuations in the markets and be ready to act at a moment's notice. Don't even think about it if you don't have a brilliant head for figures and the confidence to deal with enormous sums of money.

To become a stockbroker, you need to be qualified through the SFA's Registered Persons Examinations. Investment companies tend to recruit graduates and then train them: alternatively, you can fund the exams yourself and make the shift to the City already qualified.

Employers look for a background knowledge of stock trading. You can show your commitment by reading the *Financial Times*, by talking to people who are already in the profession and by investing small sums of your own money.

Engineer

Engineering is not top of most women's list of career options. Well, which of us would be attracted by the conventional image of greasy overalls and a spanner? But an engineer's typical tool today is a computer, not a mole wrench. And your work clothes are just as likely to be a designer suit or smart casuals as steel-capped boots and a safety helmet.

Being an engineer can involve you in anything from fuel, fibres and foods to boats, buses and bridges. You may choose to design things or processes, or you could be making things with your hands. Another option is the business end: strategic management, marketing or research and development. The area you specialise in will have specific qualifications, but all engineers require a background in science and mathematics. Teamwork, communication and problem-solving skills are also important.

Choose engineering and there are many rewards. It's a satisfying and challenging career with opportunities for self-employment and travel. How far you go will depend on your own drive and determination.

For most engineering degree courses you will normally need three scientific subjects at A level. These

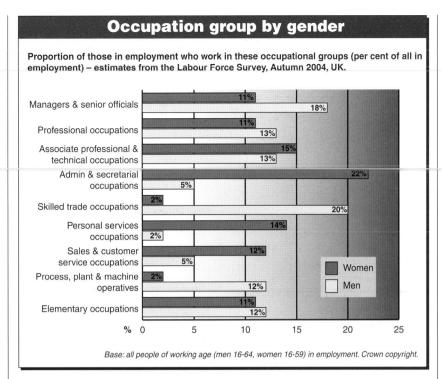

Occupation group by gender

Proportion of those in employment who work in these occupational groups (per cent of all in employment) – estimates from the Labour Force Survey, Autumn 2004, UK.

Occupational group	Women	Men
Managers & senior officials	11%	18%
Professional occupations	11%	13%
Associate professional & technical occupations	15%	13%
Admin & secretarial occupations	22%	5%
Skilled trade occupations	2%	20%
Personal services occupations	14%	2%
Sales & customer service occupations	12%	5%
Process, plant & machine operatives	2%	12%
Elementary occupations	11%	12%

Base: all people of working age (men 16-64, women 16-59) in employment. Crown copyright.

courses take between three and five years, depending on whether you want to become a Chartered or an Incorporated engineer. You can get further information from the Engineering Careers Information Service (EMTA) (0800 282167).

National AWiSE is working to promote science, engineering and technology for girls and women and to provide a network for mutual support.

Airline pilot

There aren't many jobs where you get paid for flying round the world and watching the sun rise over the Pyrenees. But, even in these days of equal opportunities, only 300 of the 13,000 UK airline pilots are women. Again, one of the reasons is that women perceive flying as a highly technical or physically demanding job. But it's more about being able to stay focused, think quickly and remain calm in very rare nerve-racking situations. And flying requires the ability to multi-task, which women are better at than men.

To become a pilot, you will need to obtain a Commercial Pilot's Licence and pass the Civil Aviation Authority's Class One medical check. To carry passengers for an airline, you'll also need the Airline Transport Pilot's Licence (ATPL). This involves passing a theory exam and clocking up 1,500 hours of flying

time. Some trainee pilots obtain full or part sponsorship from a commercial airline. Approaching private airlines directly is the best way of finding out about sponsorship and training schemes. Journals like *Flight International* or *Pilot* magazine often carry job ads from airlines such as British Airways, Virgin Atlantic, EasyJet or KLM.

You can get detailed information on qualifications from the British Airline Pilots' Association (BALPA).

■ The above information is re-printed with kind permission from handbag.com. For more information visit www.handbag.com

© 2004 handbag.com

Gender development

Information from SparkNotes

Gender is probably the most important individual difference in our society. Although the range of opportunities available to men and women continue to converge, the differences between social roles and styles remain striking. How do these differences develop? To what extent are they due to social norms and expectations or to biological differences? Definitive answers to these questions are still a long way off, but research on both the biological and social aspects of the development of gender has led to important insights. While thinking about differences between men and women, it is important to keep the distinction between sex and gender in mind. In psychology, the former is used to refer to the clear biological differences between men and women (e.g. reproductive organs, secondary sexual characteristics) and the latter is used inclusively to refer to all of the differences between men and women, including the vast amount of differences that are due to social influences.

Biology

It is clear that there are almost always striking differences between the bodies of people who have two X chromosomes and those who have an X and a Y (although there are some notable exceptions, such as when a genetic male is born with a genetic mutation that causes insensitivity to testosterone). These purely physical differences may themselves be responsible for some of the behavioural differences that are observed. For instance, the fact that women have the capacity to carry a child influences some of the activities in which they may choose to involve themselves. More interesting are the differences in behaviour that may be directly caused by sex differences in hormonal or neural systems. For instance, testosterone has been associated with aggression in males. The fact that females both have less testosterone than males and tend to be less physically aggressive suggests that hormonal differences are important determinants of behaviour.

Society

Eleanor Maccoby's research has shown that male and female children segregate themselves by sex very early in childhood. In their separate groups, they choose different kinds of games and establish different kinds of social hierarchies. Males may create larger sub-groups and engage in active and direct competition with each other. Female children, on the other hand, have been characterised as forming smaller, more intimate groups in which competition is more likely to take place on a social plane than on a physical one. While these differences may be instigated by biological differences – such as increased levels of aggression in males – they are continued and exaggerated by the social segregation of the two groups. Young girls and boys learn gender expectations and gender-appropriate behaviours by observing their parents, older children, and media representations of behaviour.

The biology vs. society debate is never a very productive one, but it continually recurs in discussions of gender differences. A useful model to follow in understanding the interaction between the two is that slight gender differences – such as boys' slight preference for active competition – may create a basis for social influences that greatly amplify those original differences. Of course, biology does not drop out of the picture entirely; it continues to influence, and be influenced by, experience.

■ The above information is reprinted with kind permission from SparkNotes LLC. For more information please visit their website at www.sparknotes.com

Division of household chores

Division of household chores between men and women, 2000/01, UK. Data are for adults 16 and over.

*Includes vehicle repair and maintenance.

Source: UK 2000 Time Use Survey, Office for National Statistics. Crown copyright.

Britain in top 10 for closing gender gap

Economic opportunity lags, but Thatcher years boost figures

Lucy Ward, Social Affairs Correspondent

The UK ranks eighth in a global league table of countries measured according to the gender gap between women and men, according to a pioneering study published yesterday (16 May 2005).

In a study of 58 countries, assessing patterns of inequality in areas including economic status, political empowerment, health and education, Britain is pipped only by the four Scandinavian countries – with Sweden at the top of the chart – and by Iceland, New Zealand and Canada.

However, the UK's high ranking in the league, produced by the Geneva-based World Economic Forum, is founded primarily on its success in educating girls to secondary and higher education level. The country also benefits from an above-average representation of women in political posts, a rating skewed by Margaret Thatcher's 11-year premiership.

Britain still lags behind on economic opportunity, a measure based largely on access to the labour market through maternity rights and availability of government-provided childcare, ranking 41st behind countries including India and Colombia.

However, some of the WEF's data, drawn from 1998 figures, does not take into account more recent improvements to Britain's maternity pay and leave.

The UK also comes 21st in the category of economic participation, measuring the proportion of women in the labour force and the gender pay gap, which is still 18 percentage points adrift in Britain 30 years after the Equal Pay Act.

Perhaps surprisingly, Britain ranks 28th on the scale of female health and well-being, a category including teenage pregnancy as well as maternal and infant mortality rates and the effectiveness of government efforts to reduce inequality.

The study, backed at its launch yesterday by the human rights lawyer Cherie Booth, wife of the prime minister, is the first attempt by the WEF to measure the status accorded to women in a range of different countries.

Pointing to a clear correlation between countries' treatment of women and their relative global competitiveness, the report warns: 'Countries that do not capitalise on the full potential of one half of their societies are misallocating their human resources and undermining their competitive potential.'

Ms Booth strongly endorsed that message, but added: 'Equality for women is an end in itself, never mind economic progress.' Regretting the loss to Labour of the Blaenau Gwent Westminster seat, which was won by the former Labour Welsh assembly member Peter Law, running as an independent, after the party imposed an all-women shortlist, Ms Booth stressed she was 'absolutely, unequivocally in favour of quotas in political empowerment terms . . . because it is actually about representation'.

Finding the five Nordic countries at the top of the table is no surprise, according to the study, which highlights their 'strongly liberal societies' with 'comprehensive safety nets' for vulnerable groups in the population and access for women to a wider spectrum of educational, political and work opportunities.

'While no country has yet managed to eliminate the gender gap, the Nordic countries have succeeded best in narrowing it and, in a very clear sense, provide a workable model for the rest of the world,' the report says.

The UK is grouped among a number of 'woman friendly' nations, including New Zealand, Canada, Germany and Australia, though several eastern European and transition countries also score highly, reflecting communist-era support for working mothers.

> *The UK ranks eighth in a global league table of countries measured according to the gender gap between women and men*

The US, in contrast, slumps in 17th place, reflecting minimal maternity rights and state childcare provision, while Switzerland, 34th, is among the lowest ranking European states, due to its poor record on higher education for women.

Augusto Lopez-Claros, chief economist at the WEF, said the league was 'not intended as a tool for embarrassing nations, but as a benchmark for improvement'.

He said the priority for closing the gap should be improving education prospects for women. Countries that do so benefit from falling adolescent pregnancy, greater income generation and associated overall wealth generation.

'The education of girls is probably the most important catalyst for change in society.'

However, the WEF faced criticisms for failing to compare like with like when it put the developing and developed worlds in one table.

17 May 2005

Men's changing lifestyles

'Early life crisis' awaits Britain's overambitious young men

Latest research from Mintel finds Britain's men wracked with worry and feeling the pressures of modern-day living. Indeed, nearly one in every ten (8%) men are 'Anxiety Ridden', finding life simply too much to handle, with this anxiety peaking at one in seven men amongst the 25- to 44-year-olds. These men worry about employment issues, time pressures and financing their desired lifestyles, which is causing them to feel stressed and overworked.

> *Despite the 'strong and silent' male typecast, only 9% of men agree that 'real men don't cry'*

'Britain's 25- to 44-year-old "Anxiety Ridden" men are going through what could be described as an "early life crisis", as opposed to a "mid life crisis". The key problem is their overambitious aspirations for themselves and their families. Over the next few years this group wants it all – better job, better home, more holidays, more time for themselves – and they hope to achieve all this while reducing their debt levels as well. Adopting more realistic ambitions would result in many men feeling happier and less stressed,' comments Angela Hughes, Consumer Research Manager.

According to Mintel's exclusive consumer research, the largest group of men are those with 'Health Woes', as one in three (34%) men fall into this group. These men seem to be preoccupied with concerns of their own personal health and that of others around them. While this group is prevalent in those aged 65 and over, well over a third of men aged 20 to 44 years old also feel this way.

A further 16% are named as 'Provision Apprehensions', who worry about both having enough provision for retirement and being able to pay for their children's education, and some 13% are 'High Life Aspirers', who feel that they do not earn enough money for the lifestyle that they would like to lead. The remaining quarter of men are 'Carefree', with no current concerns at all.

'The role of men in society has been the subject of much debate over the past three decades. It is clear that many of the changes taking place – particularly in family and working life – have challenged traditional male roles, which seems to have left many feeling they lack direction. This will of course contribute to the levels of stress and anxiety that British men are experiencing at the moment,' explains Angela Hughes.

The sharing, caring side of British men

Lager louts, boy racers and love 'em and leave 'em – there are many unpleasant male stereotypes, but it seems British men have been getting a bit of a raw deal. Nowadays they are adapting to changes in their role in society by becoming 'softer' and more in touch with their feminine side.

Exclusive consumer research shows the gap between the sexes closing, with today's men and women (just under half) being equally convinced of the importance of a lasting relationship with one partner. What is more, despite the 'strong and silent' male typecast, only 9% of men agree that 'real men don't cry' and just a quarter disagree with the statement 'I don't like to show my real feelings'.

Going green, not racing green

It seems that Britain's men are driving with a heart. While just over one in five (22%) could be described as 'Boy Racers', who enjoy a 'fast, punchy style of driving', they are far outnumbered by men with a conscience, who are worried about the pollution and congestion caused by cars (52%).

Meanwhile, nearly four in ten men (38%) agree 'a lot' that they enjoy driving, nevertheless as many as three in ten women are keen to get behind the wheel of their car.

Domestic gods

One of the biggest changes in British society has been the increase in the number of women going to work and it seems that men are up with the times as just 8% of men agree that 'a woman's place is in the home'.

Interestingly, when it comes to cleaning the house men and women seem to have similar opinions, as today nearly as many women (20%) as men (23%) agree that 'I loathe doing any form of housework'. What is more, when it comes to cooking men seem happy to step up. Indeed, men are catching up with women in terms of enjoyment of cooking with 15% of men, compared with 17% of women, definitely agreeing that they really enjoy it.

■ The above information is reprinted with kind permission from Mintel. Visit www.mintel.com for more information.

© Mintel June 2005

The great intellectual divide

By Fiona Macrae

For men, it will merely confirm what they have long suspected – and clever women will let them go on thinking it.

Psychologists have found that men have bigger brains and higher IQs than women, which may explain why chess grandmasters and geniuses are more likely to be male.

Professor Richard Lynn – who in the past has courted controversy by claiming that intelligence varies with race – says there are more men than women with higher IQs.

He and Dr Paul Irwing, a senior lecturer in organisational psychology at the University of Manchester, analysed the results of more than 20,000 reasoning tests taken by university students around the world.

Professor Richard Lynn says there are more men than women with higher IQs

---

They concluded that women's IQs are up to five points lower than men's. Their report, to be published by the *British Journal of Psychology*, is previewed in the *Times Educational Supplement*.

Dr Irwing said: 'These different proportions of men and women with high IQs may go some way to explaining the greater numbers of men achieving distinctions of various kinds of which a high IQ is required, such as chess grandmasters, Nobel prizewinners and the like.'

It could explain why more men, such as 1980 champion Fred Housego, win *Mastermind*.

Previous studies by Professor Lynn, emeritus professor of psychology at the University of Ulster, showed that girls do better in IQ tests up to the early teenage years.

But by 16, boys have drawn level, and by 21 they are on average significantly more intelligent. However, there is no need for the average man to get carried away. While they may have bigger brains, it seems men are not so clever at using them.

The extra brainpower makes men better suited to 'tasks of high complexity' but tends not to be used for everyday tasks. In fact, women can achieve more than men with the same IQ.

Dr Irwing said: 'There is some evidence to suggest that, for any given level of IQ, women are able to achieve more than men, possibly because they are more conscientious and better adapted to sustained periods of hard work.

'The small male advantage in IQ is, therefore, likely to be of most significance for tasks of high complexity such as complex problem solving in maths, engineering and physics and in areas calling for high spatial ability.'

Meanwhile, women are taking the upper hand in relationships and growing in confidence about their looks, a survey shows.

Almost two-thirds say they would ask a man to marry them rather than wait for him to pop the question, and one in three say they are comfortable chatting men up.

As for sexual attraction, women are quick to know what they want.

Twelve per cent say they know within ten seconds of starting a conversation with a man whether or not they fancy him. The majority make up their minds within five minutes. Almost half the women said they would be happy to go on holiday alone, while one in four would confidently go to a party full of strangers.

The survey of 1,500 women by Perfectil, which makes health supplements, also found that women are becoming less and less bothered by wrinkles. Two in five want to age gracefully. Asked why they thought men were becoming obsessed with their looks, 88 per cent of the women said it was because men know they cannot be complacent as their wives or girlfriends may lose interest in them.

25th August 2005

MEN CELEBRATE THEIR I.Q. SUPERIORITY...

MENSA, HERE WE COME!

MEANWHILE, WOMEN COMMISERATE...

Would you Adam and Eve it?

Men and women act differently because their brains are built differently, says Chloe Rhodes

The physical differences between men and women have long been understood, and can be traced directly to our primeval roles as hunters and child-bearers. But until recently, the many behavioural differences between them have perplexed us.

So what is it that makes women want to chat about the events of their day while men would rather reflect on theirs in silence? Why do men generally gravitate to computer and sports magazines while women prefer gossip and relationship glossies? And why do men and women often seem to want such different things from their relationships with each other?

A new BBC television series, *The Science of the Sexes*, suggests that the answers may lie in the fundamental differences in our brains – a view backed up by research published last week.

Scientists at Bath University have found that men and women feel pain in different ways, with men focusing on how to get through it as quickly as possible, and women becoming so consumed with their emotional response to an injury that they may feel it more intensely.

> *The male brain is wired to be systematic and analytical, appreciative of order and detail, while female brains are better tuned in to emotions*

In dealing with the psychological pain of divorce, the sex-divide is just as pronounced, though women are the ones most able to cope. A separate study, for the Yorkshire Building Society, revealed that women were better than men at dealing with all the stages of a break-up, 61 per cent saying that, in the first two years after a divorce, they were happier than before the relationship ended. Only 51 per cent of men felt the same way.

Clinical psychologist Dr Frank Tallis, who appears in the BBC series, says that these findings can be explained by significant differences in the brain. 'In evolutionary terms, women are designed to be sociable because they were the ones social-ising the children,' he says. 'They have communication skills that men don't have, which allow them to talk through their feelings and be comforted by their friends and family. Men are less able to make use of friendship networks and will try to minimise their emotional distress rather than trying to work through it.'

These natural advantages were found to have played an important role for the women questioned in the Yorkshire study. In the first couple of years after their divorce, they socialised more with friends, spent time with their families and received counselling or therapy. Men were more likely to seek casual sex, drink more and join a dating agency.

'You see these techniques a lot in a clinical setting,' says Dr Tallis. 'After a relationship breakdown, men tend to pursue sex as a solution, seeking a new sexual relationship to restore their self-esteem rather than taking time to reflect on why their marriage has broken down.'

Similar characteristics determine men's behaviour at the start of relationships, too. Contrary to popular belief, they are far more likely than women to fall head over heels in love, because they are more likely to follow their instinct to pursue a woman they find attractive.

'The reason some men end up with "trophy" wives is that they haven't been able to see beyond their immediate physical attraction,' says Dr Tallis. 'Women are much less likely to fall in love in this irrational way because they are programmed by evolution to look for a partner who will look after them and their children financially and emotionally; they will be looking for kindness and generosity as well as physical attractiveness.'

There is even a scientific explana-tion for stereotypical male/female behaviour. If you have ever spent an afternoon chatting on the phone while your other half watches sport, you are displaying the classic behavioural patterns of your sex. Experts say the male brain is wired to be systematic and analytical, ap-preciative of order and detail, while female brains are better tuned in to emotions.

But Dr Tallis points out that there are also social pressures that cause us to behave along gender lines. 'Men are encouraged to switch off emotion-ally. This would have been useful for early man, in combat for example, but it's not very useful for forming relationships. Women, on the other hand, are expected to be gentle and nurturing, which makes it easier for them to build bonds with other people, but leaves them needing more verbal reassurance than men.'

All of this is, of course, a dramatic simplification of the complex workings of the mind. Confusing things still further is the fact that not all women have what scientists now call a 'female brain' and not all men have a male one. Some people have 'balanced' brains, which have an equal measure of male and female characteristics, and some even have brain types opposite to their gender. There have also been links between the extreme male brain and autism,

in which the systemising power of the brain often dominates at the expense of social ability. Understanding the brain in this way is of great benefit to scientists, but even a simplified grasp of the basics may lead us all to a clearer appreciation of why we act in the way that we do – and why we often find our partners so infuriating.

Dr Tallis says the differences are just as apparent in healthy relationships as in failing ones, and that they should be embraced and understood. 'They are obviously big generalisations, but if something is generally true, it can help to prevent it from seeming personal. If an issue arises in

a relationship the man may go quiet, but this doesn't mean he is being moody or is angry – it's just that his brain works better at trying to solve the problem internally. Likewise, if the woman insists on talking, she's not just nagging for the sake of it: her instinct is telling her to communicate, and to talk about how she feels. If we consider these differences before making demands of each other, we might find that our different brains work perfectly together.'

■ *The Science of the Sexes*, broadcast on BBC1, Sunday 17 July, at 9pm.
12 July 2005

Boys, young men and gender equality

Information from XYOnline

Boys and young men are unavoidably involved in gender issues. While the term 'gender' is used often as code for women and girls, gender relations shape boys' and men's lives just as much as those of girls and women. The lives of boys and young men are structured by intersecting constructions of gender and other forms of social differentiation such as class, race and sexuality.

By Michael Flood

Certain forms of gender and sexuality are dominant (culturally celebrated and socially sanctioned) in any context, while other forms are stigmatised, silenced or punished. Boys and young men may live up to dominant forms of masculinity and heterosexuality or may resist and reject them, and they do either in the shadow of collectively structured gender relations (in media and popular culture). Constructions of gender vary among boys and young men in different cultures and countries. At the same time, there are themes that appear again and again in the lives of boys in diverse contexts.

For boys and young men, one of the most significant influences on their social and sexual interactions is male-male competition, surveillance and discipline. Many boys experience the pressure to prove themselves amongst other boys (and to a lesser extent with girls). Boys can gain status among male peers by

demonstrating their prowess in stereotypically masculine traits and pursuits, such as toughness and interpersonal dominance, sporting ability and physical skill, heterosexual sexual achievement and popularity, and humour and banter. Boys' need to prove themselves as male is shaped in part by the discrepancy between the traits associated with being young (dependent, weak and frightened) and those associated with being male (independent, strong and brave) (Lloyd 1997, p37).

Boys can gain status among male peers by demonstrating their prowess in stereotypically masculine traits and pursuits

Boys' lives at school involve a constant watching of themselves and others, an intense gendered and sexual surveillance. Boys who are perceived as 'sissies', 'wimps' or 'girlish' are punished and ridiculed. Male peer groups involve both pleasures and perils, and this same compulsory and competitive proving of one's masculinity can make them a lonely and unsupportive place (Holland, Ramazanoglu & Sharpe 1994, p14).

Research among young men finds 'a picture of complex inner-dramas of individual insecurity and low self-esteem' (Mac an Ghaill 1994, p102). Many feel shy, inadequate and unable to cope with demands of initiating and maintaining a relationship, and feel under enormous pressure from their peers (Wight 1994, p717). A central dichotomy in many young men's lives is between the projection of a public confident masculinity and their experience of private anxieties and insecurities (Mac an Ghaill 1994, p99).

When it comes to issues of sexuality and relationships, boys often distance themselves through boasting, sexual insults, silence or, most commonly, jokes (Wight 1994, p718). Boys are less likely than girls to rely on parents and teachers for information about sex and relationships, and more likely to rely on friends and television. Pornography is an important influence on boys' and young men's understandings of sexuality, and the rapid growth of the internet is likely to increase its presence (Flood and Hamilton 2003). Boys' culture often involves an ambivalence toward girls. On the one hand, boys show contempt for femaleness and the stereotypical qualities of femininity, and conflate feminine behaviour with homosexuality (Mac an Ghaill 1994, p164). On the other hand, girls are objects of sexual desire, fascination and even obsession.

Boys and young men experience pressure to gain sexual experience, as a marker of masculine status. There is pressure to have sex, from male friends, older brothers, occasionally fathers' banter, and the mass media. There is a sexual double standard, in which boys who are sexually active are judged in positive ways while girls seen to be sexually active are subject to negative labels and sanctions.

> *There is a sexual double standard, in which boys who are sexually active are judged in positive ways while girls seen to be sexually active are subject to negative labels and sanctions*

Boys learn to be stoic and inexpressive, becoming both emotionally incompetent and emotionally constipated (Doyle 1989, p158). As a result, in heterosexual relationships men often rely on women's emotional work (Strazdins & Broom 2004) and are more dependent than women on their intimate partners for emotional support. However, there is evidence of a convergence in teenage boys' and girls' understandings of and reasons for having sex.

Typical constructions of masculinity and sexuality, as well as gendered power relations, also feed into some young men's practice of sexual violence. Men who identify with traditional images of masculinity, have hostile and negative sexual attitudes towards women, see violence as manly and desirable, and believe in rape stereotypes are more likely to be sexually aggressive, sexually harassing and physically violent to women (Heise 1998, pp 227-278; O'Neil and Harway 1997, p192).

Homophobia, fear and hatred of homosexuality, exerts a fundamental influence on boys' lives and especially on male-male relations. Growing up, males are faced with the continual threat of being seen as gay and the continuous challenge of proving that they are not gay. Homophobia leads males to limit their close friendships with other males, to behave in hypermasculine and aggressive ways and to close up emotionally (Flood 1997). Homosexuality is perceived as gender betrayal, while deviation from dominant masculinity is perceived to be homosexual.

While I have identified a series of gendered and sexual patterns in boys' and young men's lives, it is critical to note also the fact of diversities among boys. In schools and other contexts, typically there are multiple and contradictory masculinities and different male peer groups with different masculine subjectivities and practices. Other forms of social differentiation such as class, race and ethnicity also structure boys' and young men's gender and sexual relations.

■ Written statement for the Commission on the Status of Women panel discussion on 'Future perspectives on the promotion of gender equality: through the eyes of young women and men', 9 March 2005. The above information is reprinted with kind permission from XYOnline. Visit www.xyonline.net for more information.

Sugar and spice?

So are girls born as sweet as fondant fancies and boys as boisterous as Labradors, or do we turn them into gender stereotypes by the way we bring them up? By Leonie Taylor

Born and bred

There's been a lot of philosophical, psychological and sociological research into whether boys and girls are created by nature or nurture, and the debate still rages.

There are, of course, chemical, hormonal, emotional and functional differences between male and female brain development. Many parents report that, even though they provide the same upbringing for their sons and daughters, their responses are different, based on gender. When given a doll, many boys choose to use it as a hammer or weapon, whereas girls tend to feed and nurture the doll.

Girls are often more able to engage in multi-task behaviour, use both sides of the brain when processing information, hear better and are more physically active; boys tend to be more spatially aware and logical, but may take more time to process and adjust to emotive information. As a parent, can you positively influence your children to go beyond stereotype?

Positive difference

Now that I have a boy (Harper, three years) and a girl (Pasha, nine months), my own exploration of gender development is well under way. Personally, I'm not fond of really blokey blokes or really girly girls. My partner (the model 'New Man') and I treat the kids the same, encouraging a certain amount of androgyny in their roles.

For instance, Harper's most enduring toys are, typically, his box of dinosaurs, his wooden railtrack and, less typically, his toy kitchen – a firm favourite with visiting toddler friends of both sexes. Strange, then, how many friends have said that they would like their boys to have a kitchen but that their partners wouldn't want their boys to have

one. Why? Surely we are doing our sons a huge favour if we equip them, as we do our daughters, with nurturing, home-making skills, so that they will eventually leave home as fully rounded, self-sufficient people, rather than the domestically useless men many of their fathers are?

As for Pasha, she loves toy cars, trains and her brother's toolkit – and I'm going to do all I can to encourage her to be as handy as possible with a screwdriver so she can make her own flat-pack furniture and put up a bookshelf as an adult. (Incidentally, Harper lovingly nurtures his ever-growing entourage of stuffed toy 'friends' while Pasha can be quite brutal with her bear – have I derailed the boy/girl continuum or is this just the age?)

The unprovable question is whether, if Harper becomes the next Jamie Oliver, and Pasha the next Jenson Button, they will have flipped the gender stereotypes because of our parenting stance or because they're simply who they are as individuals. And if Harper becomes the racing driver and Pasha the chef, are they just fulfilling their gender destinies?

Girls are often more able to engage in multi-task behaviour, boys tend to be more spatially aware and logical. Patricia Hausman, a behavioural scientist specialising in the nature and origins of human sex differences, says that the gender stereotypes are biological: 'Many argue that changes in the social environment could eliminate sex differences in interests. This perspective assumes that the "social environment" is something that Big People force on Little People. I think the Little People send signals to the Big People about what they do and do not like, and the Big People respond accordingly. Parents who buy more dolls for a daughter are probably not forcing them on her. More likely, they are reacting to observations that she did not find a toy truck particularly captivating, but lavished attention on her first doll.'

There are chemical, hormonal, emotional and functional differences between male and female brain development

---

The main thing, of course, and the aim of most good parents, is to mould confident, happy children. With both your boys and girls, encourage them to explore beyond the boundaries of Bob the Builder/ Angelina Ballerina. Even more importantly, encourage emotional and physical development in equal parts and boost self-esteem by celebrating who they are as individuals.

■ The above information is reprinted with kind permission from handbag.com. For more information visit www.handbag.com

'A Black woman took my job'

Michael Kimmel argues that it is in men's interest to work for gender equality

Over the past three generations, women's lives have been utterly and completely transformed – in politics, the military, the workplace, professions and education. But during that time, the ideology of masculinity has remained relatively intact. The notions we have about what it means to be a man remain locked in a pattern set decades ago, when the world looked very different. The single greatest obstacle to women's equality today remains the behaviour and attitudes of men.

In the mid-1970s, an American psychologist offered what he called the four basic rules of masculinity:

1 **No Sissy Stuff.** Masculinity is based on the relentless repudiation of the feminine.

2 **Be a Big Wheel.** Masculinity is measured by the size of your pay cheque, and marked by wealth, power and status. As a US bumper sticker put it: 'He who has the most toys when he dies, wins.'

3 **Be a Sturdy Oak.** What makes a man a man is that he is reliable in a crisis. And what makes him reliable in a crisis is that he resembles an inanimate object. A rock, a pillar, a tree.

4 **Give 'em Hell.** Exude an aura of daring and aggression. Take risks; live life on the edge.

The past decade has found men bumping up against the limitations of these traditional definitions, but without much of a sense of direction about where they might look for alternatives. We chafe against the edges of traditional masculinity but seem unable or unwilling to break out of the constraints of those four rules. Hence the defensiveness, the anger, the confusion that is everywhere in evidence.

Let me pair up those four rules of manhood with the four areas of

change in women's lives – gender identity, the workplace, the balance of work and family life, the sexual landscape – and suggest some of the issues I believe we are facing around the world today.

First, women made gender visible, but most men do not know they are gendered beings. Courses on gender are still populated mostly by women. Most men don't see that gender is as central to their lives as it is to women's. The privilege of privilege is that its terms are rendered invisible. It is a luxury not to have to think about race, or class, or gender. Only those marginalised by some category understand how powerful that category is when deployed against them. I was reminded of this recently when I went to give a guest lecture for a female colleague at my university. (We teach the same course on alternate semesters, so she always gives a guest lecture for me, and I do one for her.) As I walked into the auditorium, one student looked up at me and said: 'Oh, finally, an objective opinion!'

The second area in which women's lives have changed is the workplace. Recall the second rule of manhood: Be a Big Wheel. Most men derive their identity as breadwinners, as family providers. Often, though, the invisibility of masculinity makes it hard to see how gender equality will actually benefit us as men. For example, while we speak of the 'feminisation of poverty' we rarely 'see' its other side – the 'masculin-

isation of wealth'. Instead of saying that US women, on average, earn 70 per cent of what US men earn, what happens if we say that men are earning $1.30 for every dollar women earn? Now suddenly privilege is visible!

Recently I appeared on a television talk show opposite three 'angry white males' who felt they had been the victims of workplace discrimination. The show's title was 'A Black Woman Took My Job'. In my comments to these men, I invited them to consider what the word 'my' meant in that title: that they felt that the jobs were originally 'theirs'. But by what right is that 'his' job? Only by his sense of entitlement, which he now perceives as threatened by the movement towards workplace gender equality.

Violence has been part of the meaning of manhood, part of the way men have traditionally tested, demonstrated and proved their manhood

---

The economic landscape has changed dramatically and those changes have not necessarily been kind to most men. The great global expansion of the 1990s affected the top 20 per cent of the labour force. There are fewer and fewer 'big wheels'. European countries have traded growth for high unemployment, which will mean that more and more men will feel as though they haven't made the grade, will feel damaged, injured, powerless. These are men who will need to demonstrate their masculinity all over again. And here come women into the workplace in unprecedented numbers. Just when men's economic breadwinner status is threatened, women appear on the scene as easy targets for men's anger – or versions of anger. Sexual harassment, for example, is a way to remind women that they are not yet equals in the workplace, that they really don't belong there.

It is also in our interests as men to begin to find a better balance of work and family life. There's a saying that 'no man on his deathbed ever wished he had spent more time at the office'. But remember the third rule of manhood: Be a Sturdy Oak. What has traditionally made men reliable in a crisis is also what makes us unavailable emotionally to others. We are increasingly finding that the very things that we thought would make us real men impoverish our relationships with other men and with our children. Fatherhood, friendship, partnership all require emotional resources that have been, traditionally, in short supply among men, resources such as patience, compassion, tenderness, attention to process.

In the US, men become more active fathers by 'helping out' or by 'pitching in'; they spend 'quality time' with their children. But it is not 'quality time' that will provide the deep intimate relationships that we say we want, either with our partners or with our children. It's quantity time – putting in those long, hard hours of thankless, unnoticed drudge – that creates the foundation of intimacy. Nurture is doing the unheralded tasks, like holding someone when they are sick, doing the laundry, the ironing, washing the dishes. After all, men are capable of being surgeons and chefs, so we must be able to learn how to sew and to cook.

Finally, let's examine the last rule of manhood: Give 'em Hell. What this says to men is: take risks, live dangerously. And this, of course, impacts most dramatically on our bodies, sex, health and violence. Masculinity is the chief reason why men do not seek healthcare as often as women. Women perform self-

exams, seek preventive screenings, and pay attention to diet, substance abuse, far more often than men. Why? As health researcher Will Courtenay writes: 'A man who does gender correctly would be relatively unconcerned about his health and wellbeing in general. He would see himself as stronger, both physically and emotionally, than most women. He would think of himself as independent, not needing to be nurtured by others.'[1] Or, as one Zimbabwean man put it, 'real men don't get sick'.[2]

Most men don't see that gender is as central to their lives as it is to women's

---

Indeed. The ideas that we thought would make us 'real men' are the very things that endanger our health. One researcher suggested slapping a warning label on us: Caution: Masculinity May be Hazardous to your Health. A 1994 study of adolescent males in the US found that adherence to traditional masculinity ideology was associated with: being suspended from school, drinking, use of street drugs, having a high number of sexual partners, not using condoms, being picked up by the police, forcing someone to have sex.[3]

These gender-conforming behaviours increase boys' risk for HIV, STDs, early death by accident, injury or homicide. It's no exaggeration to say that the spread of HIV is driven by masculinity. HIV risk reduction requires men to take responsibility by wearing condoms. But in many cultures ignoring the health risks to

one's partner, eschewing birth control and fathering many children are signs of masculine control and power.

Finally, let me turn to what may be the single greatest public health issue of all: violence. In the US, men and boys are responsible for 95 per cent of all violent crimes. Every day 12 boys and young men commit suicide – 7 times the number of girls. Every day, 18 boys and young men die from homicide – 10 times the number of girls. From an early age, boys learn that violence is not only an acceptable form of conflict resolution but one that is admired. Four times more teenage boys than girls think fighting is appropriate when someone cuts into the front of a line. Half of all teenage boys get into a physical fight each year.

Violence has been part of the meaning of manhood, part of the way men have traditionally tested, demonstrated and proved their manhood. Without another cultural mechanism by which young boys can come to think of themselves as men, they've eagerly embraced violence as a way to become men. It would be a major undertaking to enumerate all the health consequences that result from the equation of violence and masculinity.

And just as women are saying 'yes' to their own sexual desires, there's an increased awareness of the problem of rape all over the world, especially of date and acquaintance rape. In one recent US study, 45 per cent of all college women said that they had had some form of sexual contact against their will, and a full 25 per cent had been pressed or forced to have sexual intercourse against their will. When one psychologist asked male undergraduates if they

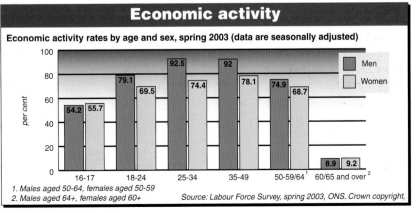

Economic activity

Economic activity rates by age and sex, spring 2003 (data are seasonally adjusted)

1. Males aged 50-64, females aged 50-59
2. Males aged 64+, females aged 60+

Source: Labour Force Survey, spring 2003, ONS. Crown copyright.

would commit rape if they were certain they could get away with it, almost 50 per cent said they would. Nearly 20 years ago, anthropologist Peggy Reeves Sanday proposed a continuum of propensity to commit rape upon which all societies could be plotted – from 'rape-prone' to 'rape-free'. (The US was ranked as a highly rape-prone society, far more than any country in Europe; Norway and Sweden were among the most rape-free.) Sanday found that the single best predictors of rape-proneness were:

1 Whether the woman continued to own property in her own name after marriage, a measure of women's autonomy.

2 Father's involvement in child-rearing; a measure of how valued parenting is, and how valued women's work.

So women's economic autonomy is a good predictor of their safety – as is men's participation in child-rearing. If men act at home the way we say we want to act, women will be safer.

And the news gets better. A 1996 study of Swedish couples found positive health outcomes for wives, husbands and children when the married couple adopted a partnership model in work-family balance issues. A recent study in the US found that men who shared housework and childcare had better health, were happier in their marriages, reported fewer psychological distress symptoms, and – perhaps most important to them – had more sex! That's right, men who share housework have more sex. What could possibly be more in men's 'interests' than that?

Another change that is beginning to erode some of those traditional 'masculine' traits, is the gradual mainstreaming of gay male culture. One of the surprise hit TV shows of the past year has been *Queer Eye for the Straight Guy*. Imagine if, 10 years ago, there'd been a TV show in which five flamboyantly gay men showed up at a straight guy's house to go through his clothing, redo his house and tell him, basically, that he hasn't a clue about how to be socially acceptable. The success of *Queer Eye* has been the partial collapse of homophobia among straight men.

And the cause of that erosion is simple: straight women, who have begun to ask straight men: 'Why can't you guys be more like gay guys?'

Rather than resisting the transformation of our lives that gender equality offers, I believe that we should embrace these changes, both because they offer us the possibilities of social and economic equality, and because they also offer us the possibilities of richer, fuller, happier lives with our friends, with our lovers, with our partners, and with our children. We, as men, should support gender equality, both at work and at home. Not because it's right and just – although it is those things. But because of what it will do for us, as men.

The feminist transformation of society is a revolution-in-progress. For nearly two centuries, we men have met insecurity by frantically shoring up our privilege or by running away. These strategies have never brought us the security and the peace we have sought. Perhaps now, as men,

we can stand with women and embrace the rest of this revolution; embrace it because of our sense of justice and fairness, embrace it for our children, our wives, our partners, and ourselves. Ninety years ago, the American writer Floyd Dell wrote an essay called 'Feminism for Men'. It's first line was this: 'Feminism will make it possible for the first time for men to be free.'

Michael Kimmel is professor of sociology at the State University of New York, Stony Brook. His books include *Manhood in America* (Free Press, 1996) and *The Gendered Society* (Oxford University Press, 2000). He is spokesperson for the National Organization for Men Against Sexism (NOMAS); www.michaelkimmel.com

References

1 WH Courtenay, 'College Men's Health: An Overview and a Call to Action', *Journal of American College Health*, Vol 46 No 6, 1998.

2 M Foreman (ed), *AIDS and Men: Taking Risks or Taking Responsibility*, Zed Books, 1999.

3 JH Pleck, FL Sonenstein, and LC Ku, 'Masculinity ideology: Its impact on adolescent males' heterosexual relationships', *Journal of Social Issues*, 49 (3), 11-29, 1993.

■ The above information is reprinted with kind permission from *New Internationalist*. Please visit www.newint.org for more information or see page 41 for address details.

Global gender inequality

Information from Oxfam

Oxfam is concerned about gender inequality because the majority of the world's poor are women: around 70 per cent of the 1.3 billion people who live in extreme poverty, on less than one dollar a day, are women and girls. Gender discrimination, or the denial of women's basic human rights, is also a major cause of poverty. Men and women experience many aspects of poverty differently and ignoring these differences risks further entrenching poverty and the subordination of women.

Unequal power relations between women and men manifest themselves in many different ways:

- Women work two-thirds of the world's working hours, and produce half of the world's food, yet earn only ten per cent of the world's income, and own less than one per cent of the world's property. (UN)
- Two-thirds of children denied primary education are girls, and 75 per cent of the world's 876 million illiterate adults are women. Every extra year a girl spends at school could reduce child mortality by ten per cent. (UN, World's Women)

- More than half a million women die in pregnancy and childbirth every year: of these deaths, 99 per cent are in developing countries. In parts of Africa, maternal mortality rates are 1 in 16. (UN, World's Women)
- Women hold only 14 per cent of parliamentary seats worldwide, and only eight per cent of the world's cabinet ministers are women. Only eleven countries have met the UN target of 30 per cent female decision-makers. (UNIFEM, Progress of the World's Women)
- Domestic violence is the biggest cause of injury and death to women worldwide. Gender-based violence causes more deaths and disability among women aged 15 to 44 than cancer, malaria, traffic accidents, and war. (World Bank Discussion Paper)

This is why gender mainstreaming, or considering gender issues in every aspect of our work, is one of Oxfam's corporate priorities. This means ensuring that both women and men are consulted, and their different needs considered in the design and implementation of programmes, to be sure that they benefit equally.

Programmes should also ensure that they promote a fairer balance of power between women and men, at household, local, national and global levels. Women should be included in decision-making processes, and civil society organisations should be supported to challenge national policies which make life harder for women and inhibit change.

Women work two-thirds of the world's working hours

In some cases Oxfam works with women's groups, to develop specific actions to help redress women's historic disadvantage. However, overcoming gender inequality and violence against women means confronting sociological and cultural barriers, and this cannot be done by working solely with women. Programme experience has shown that working with men and women together can have a more lasting impact on beliefs and behaviour, than working with women's groups alone.

At times men may feel threatened, but promoting gender equality shouldn't be seen as privileging women and disempowering men. Gender inequality and rigid gender stereotypes can often prevent a household or community from freeing itself from poverty. Ensuring equality and justice, and unlocking women's potential, is to the benefit of everyone.

- The material on this page, from http://www.oxfam.org.uk/what_we_do/issues/gender/introduction.htm is reproduced with the permission of Oxfam GB, Oxfam House, John Smith Drive, Cowley, Oxford OX4 2JY, UK, www.oxfam.org.uk. Oxfam GB does not necessarily endorse any text or activities that accompany the materials.

© Oxfam

KEY FACTS

- In 2001/02, 58 per cent of girls in their last year of compulsory education achieved five or more GCSE grades A*-C, compared with 47 per cent of boys. Forty three per cent of young women gained two or more A levels or equivalent compared with 34 per cent of young men. (page 1)

- Pupils who used computers for their school work scored higher grades in their GCSEs and national tests than those without access to computers at home, a study found. But researchers warned that children – mainly boys – who regularly played computer games achieved significantly lower grades. (page 3)

- Of 58 countries, the UK now has the 8th best record in closing the gap between the fortunes of men and women, with particular reference to economic status, political empowerment, health and education. (page 4)

- Girls outstrip boys in academic, social, emotional and physical achievement by the age of five, the first national results of the 'foundation stage profile' showed. (page 7)

- The percentage of Higher Education students who are women has been increasing steadily over recent decades and they now outnumber men: 56 per cent of HE students in 2002 were women, compared to 38 per cent in 1982. (page 8)

- Sex stereotyping still has a strong influence on course choices made by pupils: greater numbers of boys take technological and scientific subjects, while girls dominate in English and Modern Languages. (page 11)

- There are around 12.2 million women (44%) of working age in employment in the UK, compared to 15.4 million men. (page 12)

- The Glass Ceiling is an imaginary term used to describe the invisible barriers that exist within organisations and which block women from attaining senior executive positions. (page 15)

- The gender pay gap of 14.4% expresses the difference between men's and women's hourly earnings. (page 16)

- Women currently own 48% of the nation's personal wealth. (page 19)

- Even in senior positions women get paid less than men. Women do the majority of low-paid jobs. (page 20)

- 80% of girls and 55% of boys said that they would or might be interested in learning to do a non-traditional job. (page 21)

- The average score for overall job satisfaction among part-time women in the UK has fallen by eight per cent since the early Nineties and among full-time women by three per cent. (page 22)

- Nearly three in ten men (27%) would consider working in the childcare sector, and one in four boys expresses an interest in entering the 'caring' professions – yet only one in fifty childcare workers are men. (page 23)

- While one in eight girls are keen to work in the construction industry, just 1% of construction workers is female. (page 25)

- 22 per cent of women of working age work in administration and secretarial occupations, compared to just 5 per cent of men. (page 27)

- In psychology, 'sex' is used to refer to the clear biological differences between men and women (e.g. reproductive organs, secondary sexual characteristics) and 'gender' is used inclusively to refer to all of the differences between men and women, including the vast amount of differences that are due to social influences. (page 28)

- Despite the 'strong and silent' male typecast, only 9% of men agree that 'real men don't cry' and just a quarter disagree with the statement 'I don't like to show my real feelings'. (page 30)

- Professor Richard Lynn – who in the past has courted controversy by claiming that intelligence varies with race – says there are more men than women with higher IQs. (page 31)

- Scientists at Bath University have found that men and women feel pain in different ways, with men focusing on how to get through it as quickly as possible, and women becoming so consumed with their emotional response to an injury that they may feel it more intensely. (page 32)

- There is a sexual double standard, in which boys who are sexually active are judged in positive ways while girls seen to be sexually active are subject to negative labels and sanctions. (page 34)

- Most men do not know they are gendered beings. Courses on gender are still populated mostly by women. Most men don't see that gender is as central to their lives as it is to women's. (page 36)

- Women work two-thirds of the world's working hours, and produce half of the world's food, yet earn only ten per cent of the world's income, and own less than one per cent of the world's property. (page 39)

ADDITIONAL RESOURCES

You might like to contact the following organisations for further information. Due to the increasing cost of postage, many organisations cannot respond to enquiries unless they receive a stamped, addressed envelope.

Construction Industry Training Board (CITB)
Bircham Newton
KING'S LYNN
PE30 6RH
Tel: 01485 577577
Fax: 01485 577503
Email:
information.centre@citb.co.uk
Website: www.citb.co.uk
CITB-ConstructionSkills is helping to provide the fully trained and skilled workforce that the UK construction industry needs if it is to thrive now and in the future.

Department of Trade and Industry (Women and Equality Unit)
Women and Equality Unit
10 Great George Street
LONDON
SW1P 3AE
Tel: 020 7276 2021
Website:
www.womenandequalityunit.gov.uk

Equal Opportunities Commission (EOC)
Arndale House
Arndale Centre
MANCHESTER
M4 3EQ
Tel: 0161 833 9244
Fax: 0161 835 1657
Email: info@eoc.org.uk
Website: www.eoc.org.uk
The Equal Opportunities Commission is the leading agency working to eliminate sex discrimination in 21st century Britain. They campaign to:
- Close the pay gap between women and men
- Make it easier for parents to balance work with family responsibilities
- Increase the number of women in public life
- Break free of male and female stereotypes
- End sexual harassment at work
- Make public services relevant to the differing needs of men and women

- Secure comprehensive equality legislation in Europe, England, Scotland and Wales.

Girls' Schools Association
130 Regent Road
LEICESTER
LE1 7PG
Tel: 0116 2541619
Fax: 0116 2553792
Email: office@gsa.uk.com
Website: www.gsa.uk.com
The aims of the Girls' Schools Association are to:
- inform and influence national educational debate
- raise awareness of the benefits of single-sex education for girls
- promote high standards of education for girls
- support members through the provision of a broad range of services.

National Association of Citizens' Advice Bureaux
Myddleton House
115-123 Pentonville
LONDON
N1 9LZ
Tel: 020 7833 2181
Fax: 020 7833 4367
Websites: www.nacab.org.uk
www.adviceguide.org.uk
The Citizens' Advice Bureau Service offers free, confidential, impartial and independent advice. From its origins in 1939 as an emergency service during World War II, it has evolved into a professional national agency.

The New Internationalist
55 Rectory Road
OXFORD
OX4 1BW
Tel: 01865 728181
Fax: 01865 793152
Email: ni@newint.org
Website: www.newint.org
Publication on international issues. A4 40-page monthly. Circulation: 70,000 worldwide.

Oxfam GB
Oxfam House
John Smith Drive
Cowley
OXFORD
OX4 2JY
Tel: 01865 473727
Fax: 01865 312600
Email: enquiries@oxfam.org.uk
Websites: www.oxfam.org.uk
www.oxfam.org
Oxfam GB is a development, relief, and campaigning organisation dedicated to finding lasting solutions to poverty and suffering around the world.
Produces a wide range of publications. They also have the 'Oxfam Education and Resources for Schools' catalogue which outlines publications by Oxfam and other organisations.

The Work Foundation (formerly The Industrial Society)
Customer Centre
Quadrant Court
49 Calthorpe Road
Edgbaston
BIRMINGHAM
B15 1TH
Tel: 0870 165 6700
Fax: 0870 165 6701
Email:
contact@theworkfoundation.com
Website:
www.theworkfoundation.com
The Work Foundation is an independent, not-for-profit thinktank and consultancy. Through research, campaigning and practical interventions, we aim to improve the productivity and the quality of working life in the UK. We want to make our workplaces more effective, more successful and more fulfilling. We do this through research and analysis about the changing world of work; consultancy and practical interventions in UK organisations; and by influencing the public conversation about work and working life.

INDEX

ACKNOWLEDGEMENTS

The publisher is grateful for permission to reproduce the following material.

While every care has been taken to trace and acknowledge copyright, the publisher tenders its apology for any accidental infringement or where copyright has proved untraceable. The publisher would be pleased to come to a suitable arrangement in any such case with the rightful owner.

Chapter One: Gender and Education
Girls outperform boys at GCSE and A level, © Crown copyright is reprinted with the permission of Her Majesty's Stationery Office, *What is the cause of boys' underachievement?*, © Crown copyright is reprinted with the permission of Her Majesty's Stationery Office , *Computers widen gender gap*, © Guardian Newspapers Ltd 2005, *Girls-only education is shaping the future*, © Girls' Schools Association 2005, *Single-sex teaching*, © Crown copyright is reprinted with the permission of Her Majesty's Stationery Office, *Are girls short-changed in the co-ed classroom?*, © Girls' Schools Association 2005, *The achievement gap*, © Telegraph Group Ltd 2005, *Gender and achievement*, © Crown copyright is reprinted with the permission of Her Majesty's Stationery Office, *Equality issues in education*, © Equal Opportunities Commission.

Chapter Two: Gender and Employment
Key facts on women in the labour market, © Crown copyright is reprinted with the permission of Her Majesty's Stationery Office, *Sex Discrimination and Equal Pay Acts*, © Equal Opportunities Commission, *Positive discrimination and positive action*, © Citizens' Advice Bureau, *Breaking through the glass ceiling*, © University of Westminster, *What is the pay gap and why does it exist?*, © Crown copyright is reprinted with the permission of Her Majesty's Stationery Office, *Gender pay gap wider than previously thought*, © Incomes Data Services, *Women at the top*, © Crown copyright is reprinted with the permission of Her Majesty's Stationery Office, *Women to hold 60% of UK wealth by 2025*, © Centre for Economics and Business Research Ltd 2005, *Do our daughters really have the world at their feet?*, © The Work Foundation 2005, *Free to choose?*, © Equal Opportunities Commission 2005, *Women's job satisfaction*, © Telegraph Group Ltd 2005, *Jobs for the boys?*, © Equal Opportunities Commission 2005, *Sisters are 'building it for themselves'*, © CITB-ConstructionSkills, *Jobs for the girls*, © 2004 handbag.com.

Chapter Three: Gender and Society
Gender development, © 2005 SparkNotes LLC all rights reserved, *Britain in top 10 for closing gender gap*, © Guardian Newspapers Limited 2005, *Men's changing lifestyles*, © Mintel June 2005, *The great intellectual divide*, © 2005 Associated Newspapers Ltd, *Would you Adam and Eve it?*, © Telegraph Group Ltd 2005, *Boys, young men and gender equality*, © Michael Flood 2005, *Sugar and spice?*, © 2004 handbag.com, *'A Black woman took my job'*, © Copyright 2004 New Internationalist Publications Ltd. All rights reserved, *Global gender inequality*, © Oxfam.

Photographs and illustrations:
Pages 1, 26, 38: Don Hatcher; pages 4, 23, 34, 39: Simon Kneebone; pages 11, 15, 31: Angelo Madrid; page 19: Bev Aisbett.

Craig Donnellan
Cambridge
January, 2006